LABOR ON THE LINE

LABOR ON THE LINE

Justice at Work on Assam
Tea Plantations

Anna-Lena Wolf

ILR PRESS

AN IMPRINT OF CORNELL UNIVERSITY PRESS   ITHACA AND LONDON

Thanks to generous funding from the Swiss National Science Foundation, the ebook editions of this book are available as open access volumes through the Cornell Open initiative.

First published 2025 by Cornell University Press

Librarians: A CIP catalog record for this book is available from the Library of Congress.

ISBN 9781501783364 (hardcover)
ISBN 9781501783371 (paperback)
ISBN 9781501783395 (pdf)
ISBN 9781501783388 (epub)

GPSR EU contact: Sam Thornton, Mare Nostrum Group B.V., Mauritskade 21D, 1091 GC, Amsterdam, NL, gpsr@mare-nostrum.co.uk.

https://doi.org/10.7298/s2sn-3g55

जूना और बिनिता के लिए

Contents

Acknowledgments ix

Abbreviations xii

Note on Translation and Transliteration xiii

Introduction: Justice Works! 1

1. Scales of Justice Within and Beyond Plantation "Enclaves" 25

2. Living from the Tea Leaves 39

3. Why Tea Plantation Laborers Do (Not) Rebel 56

4. Justice and Categories of Collective Identification 72

5. Bungalow Doctrines 88

Conclusion: Workings of Justice 108

Notes 115
References 121
Index 129

Acknowledgments

This book would not have been published without the help of many people. Not all of them can be named here, especially because pseudonyms have been used for many interlocutors. Nonetheless, above all, my thanks go to the families on the tea plantations who allowed me to stay with them and to the numerous people from the plantations who invited me into their homes, allowed me to join them for work and leisure activities, and shared their stories and lives with me. I am inexpressibly thankful to Binita, who grew up on a tea plantation and who helped me get used to life on the plantations, spent many hours explaining to me her point of view on my experiences during fieldwork, and read and commented on many early drafts of this book. Binita has an extraordinary desire to learn more. Her nonconformist determination has inspired me. The world needs people like Binita in important positions. I owe my thanks to Juna, who always welcomed me in front of the firepit in her kitchen for a pot of tea. Juna's wisdom, warmth, and joy for life are an incomparable treasure. I regret that she will never be able to read this book because life did not give her the opportunity to learn to read. I wish the many scholars of this world, including me, had even a spark of her world-changing wisdom. I am thankful for all the things that I learned from Juna. Equally, I am grateful to Rimti for taking me to work, walking me around the plantation, and sharing many insights about life and work with me. Rimti's eagerness and rebelliousness impressed me deeply. I am also thankful to Alex, Angansri, Anita, Anjana, Arti, Ashin, Ashok, Hiramoni, Kathrina, Klara, Mahipal, Mansuk, Manjushah, Melkhas, Petrus, Richek, Rita, Sarita, Shuklal, Simon, and Sunita.

At an early stage of my research, I stayed at the Jawaharlal Nehru University in Delhi. During that time, academics, human rights lawyers, and activists inspired my thinking and helped me in many ways. I am particularly thankful to Anant Kumar Asthana, Amit Prakash, Colin Gonsalves, Franscesca Feruglio, Jayshree Satpute, Meha Khanduri, and most importantly Pratiksha Baxi.

In Assam, Adivasi activists helped me with my fieldwork in various ways. I am thankful to Raphael Kujur, and Wilfred Topno for sharing their valuable knowledge with me. From the academic circles around the Tata Institute of Social Sciences in Guwahati, I am grateful for the rich discussions with Dolly Kikon, Mirza Zulfiqur Rahman (IIT Guwahati), R. K. Debbarma, Sanjay (Xonzoi) Barbora, Trishna Gogoi, Virginius Xaxa, and Yengkhom Jilangamba who helped me to gain a better knowledge about Assam and its tea plantations. My heartfelt thanks go to Trishna and her family, who have shown me more hospitality than one could ever imagine. It is such a joy that we met and were able to walk a part of the way together in Assam. Thank you for everything!

For their guidance and feedback at various stages of research and writing, I express my deep thankfulness to my mentor Julia Eckert and her sit-in colloquium group. It was a true pleasure to work with Julia Eckert. She has profoundly shaped my perspective on India, and I am deeply grateful for the countless hours we spent discussing my research. I sincerely appreciate her exceptionally astute criticism, combined with her genuine warmth. For further guidance and feedback on parts of the book, I thank Andrew Tony-Odigie, Edda Rohrbach, Gabriel Zimmerer, Gaurav J. Pathania, Johanna Mugler, Johannes Quack, Justine Le Goff, Laura Affolter, Luisa Piart, Miriam Wenner, Rana Behal, Ravi Ahuja, Sabine Friebolin, Sandra Bärnreuther, Sanjib Baruah, Sarah Besky, Sarah Ewald, and Selina Abächerli. I would like to express special gratitude to Sandra Bärnreuther for her countless support, much like a Didi ("older sister"), in helping me navigate the academic world. Her exceptional ability to listen and ask insightful, well-founded questions has been a constant source of inspiration for my anthropological work. I am grateful to Olaf Zenker for his belief in the success of this book. Without his support, the book would surely not have been published by Cornell. I also thank Olaf Zenker and the Political and Legal Anthropology Network for all the inspiring conversations about the book.

This book started at the University of Bern. My fieldwork was funded by the Heinrich Boell Foundation and by the University of Bern's Faculty of Humanities fieldwork grants. I thank the foundation and the faculty for their trust in my project and their generous financial support. The many discussions with Axel Harneit-Sievers and Caroline Bertram from the Delhi office of the Heinrich Boell Foundation were fertile and enjoyable. Caro's and my shared love for India has brought us especially close in recent years. Thank you for our special friendship.

Parts of chapter 2 of the book were first published in *Anthropology and Humanism* in 2023 under the title "'It Would Taste Better with Sugar'—Navigating Deprivation and Confidence in Everyday Life on a Tea Plantation in Assam." An earlier version of chapter 1 appeared in the 2022 article "Beyond 'Enclaves': Post-Colonial Labor Mobility to and from Assam Tea Plantations" in *Anthropology of Work Review*. Parts of chapter 4 were published in the article "'No Justice—No Rest!': How Activist Conceptions of Justice Influence Categories of Collective Identification among Tea Plantation Laborers in Assam" published in 2023 in the *Zeitschrift für Ethnologie | Journal of Social and Cultural Anthropology*. I am extremely thankful to Jim Lance and the ILR Board from Cornell University

Press and the two anonymous reviewers of the book manuscript for their helpful comments, suggestions, and guidance.

Finally, I would like to express my thanks to my dear family. I thank my parents, Margret and Josef; my brother, Benjamin; and my beloved sons, Adam and Amadeo, for supporting me emotionally, although my path as an anthropologist remains puzzling to them.

Abbreviations

AASAA	All Adivasi Students' Association of Assam
ACMS	Assam Chah Mazdoor Sangha
AITUC	All India Trade Union Congress
APPL	Amalgamated Plantations Private Limited
APTUC	Assam Provincial Trade Union Congress
ATTSA	All Assam Tea Tribes Student Association
BLF	Bought Leaf Factory
CCPA	Consultative Committee of Plantation Associations
CTC	Crush, Tear, Curl
INTUC	Indian National Trade Union Congress
NGO	Nongovernmental Organization
OBC	Other Backward Classes
PLA	Plantations Labour Act
SC	Scheduled Castes
ST	Scheduled Tribes

Note on Translation and Transliteration

All the interviews that were conducted in Hindi were translated into English by me. The translation and textualization of the interviews followed standard orthography, which is guided by principles of written script, while no attention was paid to the peculiarities of spoken language, such as prosodic or paralinguistic features (Kowal and O'Connell 2012, 438–441). If the English translation of a word or passage in an interview varied significantly from the literal translation, the original Hindi word or passage is given italicized in brackets afterward. Hindi words are transliterated, following rules guided by the International Alphabet of Sanskrit Transliteration. The International Alphabet of Sanskrit Transliteration rules are adjusted to the peculiarities of the Hindi language. *Chandrabindu* and *Anusvar* are transliterated with *n* for reasons of readability. Personal names, place names, and common concepts (e.g., *dharma*) in Hindi are incorporated into the running text without diacritical signs.

LABOR ON THE LINE

JUSTICE WORKS!

I entered the green wooden front door to Anjali's brick house.[1] Anjali lived with her in-laws in one of the lower labor lines of Dolani Tea Estate.[2] A few chickens ran across the front garden, which was fenced off from the street with bamboo. Directly behind her house, the garden section of the plantation began. Anjali's father-in-law was sitting in the living room. He told me that he came to Assam from Jharkhand in 1972, when there was a severe drought in Central India and farmers were hardly getting any crops. In the beginning he had been very scared to move to the unknown state of Assam. Initially, his family members thought they would only come for a few years to earn some money before returning to Jharkhand. But in the end, they stayed. Meanwhile, he emphasized, Assam has become their home (*ghar*). They still travel to Jharkhand once a year to visit their relatives there, but they would not consider returning permanently anymore. Anjali came out of the kitchen with three fragrant cups of tea and sat down with us. Anjali was twenty-six years old when I met her in 2015. She had two daughters, who then were seven and four years old. Her husband worked in the tea factory. She went to first grade but quickly dropped out of school because she was afraid of the teacher. At the age of fourteen, she had started working as a temporary laborer on the plantation. After her marriage, she "inherited" her mother-in-law's permanent position on the plantation.[3] As we sipped our hot tea, Anjali became troubled. She had heard rumors that the food rations, which laborers got as part of their salary as weekly nonmonetary benefits, would be repealed. "That's about the worst thing I can imagine," she commented anxiously.

Some four hundred kilometers east of Dolani Tea Estate, the head office of the Assam Chah Mazdoor Sangha (ACMS) was located. On its website, the single most important trade union working on behalf of tea plantation workers in Assam describes its main objectives as "eliminating social, political and economic exploitation and inequality." In 2015, I visited the ACMS head office in Dibrugarh. When I moved into the building, it looked surprisingly small and dilapidated to me. There were two offices on the left side hosting the president in the back and the general secretary in the front as well as two administrative offices on the right side. An administrative staff welcomed me and asked me to wait for the general secretary in one of the administrative offices. After an hour or so, another staff member sneaked into the office saying that Dileswar Tanti, the general secretary, had arrived. They led me into his office. Tanti sat behind his desk. He was busy signing documents while I entered his office and did not make an effort to greet me. I asked him nonetheless about the trade union's agenda. He told me: "We deal with the workers' problems mainly . . . we look after the implementation of labor laws, such as the Minimum Wages Act or the Plantations Labour Act." The then–last wage agreement for tea plantation laborers in Assam had been settled on February 26, 2015.[4] I asked Tanti why the ACMS did not support the introduction of the statutory minimum wage even after the Assamese government had supported it (see *Times of India* 2015). He replied that the minimum wage was the government's responsibility, not the responsibility of the trade union. He stated, "I voted for Rs. 115. Rs. 169 has no basis because the industries are so different and in the tea industry, there are many other obligations that are not there in other industries. Rs.115 is according to the economic capacity of the industry."

Activists working on behalf of Assam tea plantation workers had organized several protests against the "illegal" wage agreement below the statutory minimum wage and the trade union's agreement to it. When the ACMS president was visiting a branch office in a district capital in Assam, activists organized a protest in front of the branch office. They wanted to lock the trade union office with a huge lock from the outside to pass the message that that trade union is useless. When the trade union president realized the activists' plan, he escaped the branch office before they were able to lock it. The activists got so angry when they saw the president escaping that they broke everything down in the office. One of the activists who was imprisoned after the protest went violent later commented, "We're not actually thugs (*ham log to yahan marne-pitne ke lie nahin hain*), are we? Our aim is to defend ourselves against the conspiracy between trade union and management. The president represents the union. We thought how he can just run away. I got over-sentimental. Our motto is that 115 is illegal and we demand 169."

Not far from the district office, where the protest had taken place, Mr. Puzaris and his wife lived in a manager bungalow on a privately owned tea estate. Mr. Puzaris had studied law before becoming a tea plantation manager thirty-eight years earlier. His father had been working for the Indian government as a tax officer. I asked Mr. Puzaris how he got involved in the tea business. He said that he grew up in the area around Jorhat where many tea gardens were located. Since childhood he had been attracted to the "tea garden life," which he found so different because along with the establishment of the tea industry the British had brought their "lordly lifestyle to the tea gardens." While we were sitting on the veranda drinking tea, Mr. Puzaris handed me a copy of the Plantations Labour Act and commented, "This is a given fact for us." Mr. Puzaris argued that the laborers got the minimum wage already when all provisions they received were included in the calculation. He saw it as his "duty to protect" the tea industry by keeping the wages affordable.

Academics and activists alike have criticized the conditions on postindependence tea plantations in Assam as "modern-day slavery" (e.g., Ray 2016). However, when I conducted ethnographic fieldwork on Assam's tea plantations between 2014 and 2017, I found that tea plantation laborers and trade unionists formed surprising alliances with tea planters around their everyday conceptions of justice, as the ethnographic snippets above, which introduce differently positioned actors on Assam tea plantations, illustrate.[5] When fundamental changes were appearing in the political economy of tea production in India (see below), laborers, trade unionists, and managers, in one way or another, remained in favor of an "old-style" plantation economy based on paternalist dual wage structures that have been criticized as a form of bondage by academics and activists. Why did tea laborers and trade unionists support the maintenance of an exploitive labor regime, one that had been created initially to develop a totalitarian work environment during the colonial establishment of industrial tea production in Assam?

To answer this puzzling question that haunted me while I conducted fieldwork in India, I develop the concept *justice at work* over the course of the book. *Justice at work* has two layers of meaning. First, it analyzes how justice is conceptualized, negotiated, and transformed in the everyday lives of differently positioned actors—including tea laborers, trade unionists, activists, and tea planters—"at work" on Assam's tea plantations. Second, *justice at work* is based on the premise that everyday conceptualizations of justice maintain, enhance, limit, or "work at" differently positioned actors' odds to act, and vice versa.[6] Before elaborating the concept *justice at work* in detail, I illustrate in the next section how matters of justice have been addressed in research on industrial tea production on plantations and beyond to specify in the sections afterward how *justice at work* builds on these previous studies.

Matters of Justice in Tea Ethnographies

There are a couple of studies on plantation economies that have addressed matters of justice implicitly or explicitly (Banerjee 2017; Bass 2013; Besky 2014; Bourgois 1989; Bhowmik 2011; Chatterjee 2001; Chaudhuri 2013; Ives 2017; Jegathesan 2019; Raj 2022; Sen 2017; Stoler 1985; Willford 2014). I discuss three paradigmatic concepts (tripartite moral economy, *swaccha vyāpār*, and *poiēsis* of desire) developed in tea ethnographies to illustrate how matters of justice have been studied in tea ethnographies to then show how *justice at work* builds on these previous studies.

Justifiably the most widely received empirical study dealing with matters of justice on tea plantations is the ethnography *The Darjeeling Distinction* by Sarah Besky (2014). Besky introduces fair trade ("justice as fairness"), geographical indication ("justice as property"), and the Gorkhaland movement ("justice as sovereignty") as three visions for a more just plantation life.[7] The author criticizes all three visions of justice because they rely on what she calls a "Third World agrarian imaginary" (29). In this imaginary, the plantations in the postcolonial world are stripped of their colonial heritage of global capitalist labor exploitation and are whitewashed as "tea gardens" or "farms," where people supposedly live and work traditionally and happily in harmony with nature. Besky's main argument is that none of the three visions of justice critically questions the plantation economy "despite their appeals to justice" (29). Instead, the three visions reinterpret the plantation economy in a new light—obscuring its exploitative history and present and making it more profitable for new markets by "imagining injustice as something that can be overcome *within the context of the plantation itself*" (20; emphasis in original). None of the visions for justice, according to Besky, considers the tea plantation workers' perspectives.

Besky uses the concept of a "tripartite moral economy" to capture laborers' idea(l)s of just labor conditions and relations as a reciprocity between management, labor, and the agro-environment—three unequal partners that cohabit the same space (32).[8] The tripartite moral economy is a multispecies relationship between humans and nonhumans on plantations or a system of mutual obligations between laborers, planters, and the environment. For Besky, laborers' nostalgia of a bygone tripartite moral economy, which laborers locate historically before the 1990s, when most tea plantations in Darjeeling turned toward Fair Trade, organic, or other certifications, is an expression of laborers' critique of the status quo of plantation economies as well as a vision of a better future.

While scholars of moral economy such as E. P. Thompson and James C. Scott have focused on resistance in form of organized revolts or everyday forms of resistance, Besky sees a more complicated articulation of resistance in laborers' concept of a tripartite moral economy: When wallowing in memories of past stability, plantation women were *actually* criticizing the plantation economy and "envisioning a more stable future for their children" (85).

Similarly, the ethnography *Everyday Sustainability* by Debarati Sen (2017) looks at "justice imaginaries" of Nepali tea workers in relation to and in conflict with Fair Trade initiatives in Darjeeling.[9] Unlike Besky, Sen includes smallholder women tea farmers who grow tea autonomically on a small plot of land outside the plantations in relation to women tea plantation workers. On the background of Fair Trade's declared aim to empower marginalized producers, Sen asks "how intended beneficiaries of the global Fair Trade movement understood the value of Fair Trade in the context of their situated identity struggles and their everyday entrepreneurialism to gain social and economic justice" (127–128). Instead of portraying women tea workers as passive recipients of global sustainability initiatives, Sen argues that women tea farmers showed both skepticism and creativity in engagement with Fair Trade (4). Women tea farmers, on the one hand, criticized Fair Trade for entrenching the "power of patriarchal production systems through deceptive language of women's empowerment and inclusion" (22). On the other hand, women tea farmers appropriated Fair Trade to their own justice imaginaries in "gendered projects of value" (12). By gendered project of value, Sen describes, for instance, informal networks and collectives (*ghumāuri*), new categories of collective identification such as "housewife-entrepreneurs," and women's local concepts of fair trading such as *swaccha vyāpār*, which subvert local patriarchal hegemonies and logics of capital accumulation.

Swaccha vyāpār is a "distinct Nepali iteration of Fair Trade that incorporates awareness of gender hierarchies" (128). Sen observed that women tea farmers use the notion of *swaccha vyāpār* to rhetorically juxtapose it with Fair Trade. According to Sen, saying that Fair Trade was not *swaccha vyāpār* was a way to criticize that those who profited from the Fair Trade label were male middlemen and not woman tea workers and a way to criticize the economistic reductionism of Fair Trade. While the Fair Trade certifiers came with ideas of liberal gender equality in the form of representation that ignores local realities, the women found ways to "substantiate and advance their own projects of justice" (141) simultaneously through and against Fair Trade. Sen illustrates how *swaccha vyāpār* and other gendered projects of value became a powerful tool for Nepali women tea farmers' justice imaginaries in Darjeeling.[10]

Taking a slightly different conceptual emphasis, Mythri Jegathesan (2019, 10–11), in her ethnography *Tea & Solidarity*, examines Hill Country Tamil tea plantation workers' desires for dignity in the context of "Sri Lanka's postwar calls for political reform and economic development." Jegathesan chose a feminist, humanistic, and decolonial approach that she considers more commensurable and in solidarity with the way in which workers themselves want to be studied in comparison to "primarily male-focused, structural, economic, and rights-based lenses" on Hill Country Tamil plantation workers (201).[11] She argues "that women workers' desire for dignity and better futures have the potential to productively disrupt and positively transform the story of Ceylon tea and the industry's ethical future" (11–12). To explain how desires operate as "active sites of social change and disruption" (23), Jegathesan develops the concept "*poiēsis* of desire." The author borrows the term *poiēsis* from Martin Heidegger who, according to Jegathesan, understands it as "bringing forth" or shifting the structures that enclose desire (38). By "desire" Jegathesan describes moving "past what we want and in relation to what we have" (39). At the core of the *poiēsis* of desire is what Jegathesan calls "unbecoming labor" (21). Hill Country Tamils in Sri Lanka can fulfill their desire for dignified recognition by unbecoming labor according to Jegathesan. Unbecoming labor is a polyvalent "process of becoming a collective something not yet known . . . and not yet complete" (39) but implies "desiring to delink from their heritage of coolie labor" and aspiring "to work anywhere but on the tea plantations" (201).

The concepts of the tripartite moral economy, *swaccha vyāpār*, and *poiēsis* of desire are attempts to represent tea laborers' perspectives, interpret them as forms of critique of hegemonic systems, and contrast them with other imaginaries of justice. The tripartite moral economy and the *poiēsis* of desire constitute a critique of neocolonial exploitative plantation economies. Justice for laborers is imagined to be gained exclusively outside plantation economies. Desires are seen to be fulfilled by unbecoming plantation labor. The tripartite moral economy and *swaccha vyāpār* constitute critical evaluations of global sustainability initiatives such as Fair Trade. In the laborers' tripartite moral economy, Fair Trade is seen as an amoral *bisnis* model of plantation economy, in which *bisnis*-men do not care about laborers but are only interested in extracting from land and labor (Besky 2014, 62). Contrasting *swaccha vyāpār* with Fair Trade is a means to criticize Fair Trade for not advancing gender justice for women in their local contexts. All three concepts portray tea laborers' perspectives as rebellions against hegemonic structures of capitalism, patriarchy, and neocolonialism. The laborers' perspective is contrasted with other concepts of justice such as Fair Trade. For Besky, Fair Trade creates a self-image of providing fairer trading conditions on a global market while *actually* undermining state welfare initiatives by the Indian state. In contrast, the laborers' tripartite moral economy is a "complicated articulation of resistance" in which "workers are keenly aware that in the market for justice, the plantation is not going anywhere" (85). In the following section, I will outline on how my understanding of justice is related to concepts such as tripartite moral economy, gendered projects of value like *swaccha vyāpār*, or *poiēsis* of desire.

Justice as What People Consider to Be Due to Someone

During my fieldwork, I encountered laborers with various perspectives and desires, but I was struck by the prevalence of laborers' "declarations of dependence" (Ferguson 2013) and the alliances they had built with trade unionists and tea managers (sometimes against activists) in maintaining the industrial tea production on Assam's plantations rather than questioning it. To make sense of these unanticipated alliances between laborers, trade unionists, and tea managers, I develop the concept *justice at work*. It builds on an analytical justice category I developed elsewhere together with Olaf Zenker in order to pluralize notions of justice. We suggest defining justice as "matters of concern about what is due to different (kinds of) subjects according to relatively stable and impartial values and norms to be enacted by specifiable and thus responsible agents" (Zenker and Wolf 2024, 8). *Subjects of justice* are those to whom justice is due. What is due is called *objects of justice*. *Responsible agents of justice* are those who are imagined to be responsible to implement objects of justice (Zenker and Wolf 2024, 6–9).[12]

My ambition to pluralize notions of justice by suggesting an analytical definition of justice applicable to different situations and people started during my research on Assam tea plantations. I became interested in studying matters of justice on Assam tea plantations when I was working with a human rights organization in Delhi in 2014. Some of the international activists were founding an organization dedicated to bringing justice to marginalized people in India, including Assam tea plantation laborers.[13] The activists put me in touch with activists in Assam who allowed me to stay for some time in a training center on a plantation. Initially, my research project resembled the activists' presuppositions, their perception of tea laborers, and their objectives. In an unpublished fieldwork summary on September 19, 2015, I wrote that my research project was about "how the exclusion of tea plantation workers in Assam is administered" and "how the administration of exclusion is subverted" by activist groups. This description mirrored the activists' two related main objectives: first, to display the tea plantation laborers as one of the most discriminated-against subaltern groups, and second, to show how their activism successfully helped to overcome tea workers' marginalization. After spending some time with both activists and laborers, I increasingly felt that there was a discrepancy between the "justice" that activists wanted to bring close to laborers and laborers' different perspectives on justice in relation to trade unionists and tea planters. I started to see the activists' perspective as one among other perspectives that was driven by their own conceptions of justice, which overlapped with the multiplicity of workers' perspectives on matters of justice only to a certain extent.

Since I felt that laborers had everyday conceptions of justice even though they were not using the term *justice* or a local translation of it most of the time, it became obvious to me that I must have had an implicit concept of justice in mind to feel that way. How could I have otherwise felt that they had conceptions of justice when they did not use the word *justice* literally to express them? Reflecting on my own implicit notions of justice "at work" within myself, I realized that justice for me was in a nutshell about what people considered to be due to them and others.[14] This definition of justice can be useful to look at multiple ideas of justice because it does not normatively predetermine "objects of justice" or *what* people consider to be due to them and others.

My understanding of justice is related to but not identical to previous concepts such as tripartite moral economy, gendered projects of value like *swaccha vyāpār*, or *poiēsis* of desire. Besky uses the concept "tripartite moral economy" to analyze marginalized tea laborers' alternative views about what constitutes a "moral" or "fair" economy in contrast to other justice imaginaries such as Fair Trade.[15] I use the concept of justice to explore, compare, and relate differently positioned actors' perspectives on what people consider to be due to them and others. Therefore, I use justice as an analytical concept to describe both "subaltern" and elitist perspectives alike. Furthermore, ideas about what is due to whom are related to but not limited to economic questions. For instance, Sen's gendered projects of value are directed toward the empowerment of women. Thereby, the subjects of justice concerned in gendered projects of value are women, and the object of justice is predefined: Gender justice is what is due to women. In the suggested analytical definition of justice, the scope of who is considered a subject of justice is broader. Subjects of justice include tea laborers, trade unionists, activists, and tea planters. Similarly, the object of justice is less targeted. I introduce different objects of justice such as maintaining the tea industry, affirmative action, and minimum wages that change over time. Dignity was not only a desire for tea laborers in Assam but also something they considered to be due to them. However, Jegathesan's understanding of desire as moving "past what we want and in relation to what we have" (Jegathesan 2019, 39) is different from considerations about what is due to someone. On the one hand, the idea of what is due to someone implies an obligation—one is entitled to claim what is due to oneself or others. Desire as wanting something does not necessarily imply obliging somebody. A person can want something without feeling entitled to it.[16] On the other hand, the idea of "moving past" as central to desire does not necessarily apply to concepts of justice. What is due to somebody can already be in place and does not necessarily need to go beyond the status quo.

To sum up, justice as what people consider to be due to them and others involves different subjects of justice to whom a multiplicity of objects of justice are considered to be due by different responsible agents of justice. Therefore, justice is a suitable analytical lens to understand differently positioned actors and how their various conceptualizations of justice are related to one another. However, justice imaginaries are not immutable, clear-cut, and unambiguous in the social context in which they appear; they should be understood as heuristic devices developed for the purpose of analysis to better understand what people consider to be due to them and others.

Justice at Work

Building on the suggested analytical concept of justice, *justice at work* is about what justice does "as an idea or a practice" (Brunnegger 2019, 4). It analyzes how everyday conceptualizations of justice maintain, enhance, limit, or "work at" differently positioned actors' odds to act, and vice versa. Odds to act have been discussed regarding the question of the relationship between structure and agency. Some positions rather focus on how structures predispose and thus reproduce agency. For instance, Ann Stoler (1985, viii) in her study on the development of plantations in Sumatra under Dutch colonial rule studied "how and why certain social hierarchies, economic inequalities, and political privileges were created, made to appear immutable, contested, and reproduced." Stoler argued that it "includes more than the imposition of a dominant ideology expressing and serving the interests of a ruling class but 'its acceptance as "normal reality" or "commonsense" by those in practice subordinated to it'" (Williams 1980, 118; quoted in Stoler 1985, 8–9). Another example of a stronger focus on structural constraints is Jayaseelan Raj's analysis of transformations in plantation economies in the South Indian state of Kerala in the context of the Indian tea crisis in his book *Plantation Crisis*. For Raj (2022, 14), the tea crisis is a "situated event"— at the same time a situation or "the context in which the event takes place" and an event that "restructures the context."

Other positions in anthropology have placed a strong focus on nonhuman and decentralized agency (e.g., Latour 2005; Viveiros de Castro 1998; Holbraad 2012; Haraway 1991), which also resonates with studies on plantation economies that emphasize networks between human and more-than-human actors like tea plants (e.g., Barua 2024; Besky 2014; Kumpf 2020). For instance, Sarah

Besky's tripartite moral economy includes the more-than-human agro-environment among other actors such as tea plantation workers and managers. In these posthuman approaches, the singularity of human agency has been dispersed to decenter humans and redistribute capabilities to act beyond humans.

Some positions place a stronger focus on specifically human agency and freedoms to act despite structural constraints. Supurna Banerjee (2017, 157) in her ethnography of activism and agency on tea plantations in Dooars in the Northeast Indian state of West Bengal, for example, wants to overcome binaries of agency and victimhood by asking "what sort of agents the women can be despite their subordination." Agency is articulated for Banerjee in her research field either by choice and decision-making or by resistance. An agential choice may be seen in a woman laborer's preference not to remarry, thereby undermining social norms and expectations of how she as a woman should behave. Agency as resistance is shown, for instance, in delaying work or cheating the management. Resistance can also be seen in practices such as gossiping or critiquing the system through carnivalesque performances or critical poetry and songs recited in public events. These acts of resistance, according to Banerjee, are a way to critique an unequal and oppressive system and "serve as means for the women to achieve their own ends, however limited these might be" (156). Following Banerjee, my position is also a stronger focus on specifically human agency and freedoms to act despite structural constraints that Anthony Giddens (1984, 9) has pointedly called humans' capability to act or have acted differently while nonetheless acknowledging that agency is structurally situated and constrained (see also Zenker 2018).

Everyday conceptions of justice are part of the structures that shape possibilities to act (differently), and they are simultaneously transformed by people's actions. While previous studies have situated agency almost exclusively in acts of resistance and emancipation from oppressive systems, I consider agency in both choices for and against oppressive systems. Seeing people's agency only in acts of resistance, while excluding people's "declarations of dependence" (Ferguson 2013) as agential choices, may amount to giving voice to tea laborers, not in order to make their own words heard "but to make their words address our own concerns, and to render their figures in our own self image" (O'Hanlon 1988, 210) or to render their figures in our own justice imaginaries instead of their own.

In the book, based on my empirical findings, I develop four workings of justice: justice on scales, justice in context, justice in transition, and justice in conflict. *Justice on scales* implies that justice imaginaries work differently on different scales such as plantations, nation-states, or globally (see chap. 1). When justice is upscaled, subjects and objects of justice are less clearly definable and therefore more difficult to approach. When justice is downscaled, for instance to the plantation scale, subjects and objects of justice are more easily identifiable, but it is less likely that the identified agents of justice have the capacity to implement what is due to different subjects of justice. *Justice in context* illustrates that justice imaginaries work different in different spaciotemporal contexts (see chap. 3). While justice imaginaries may appear structure preserving in one context, they may be structure undermining in other contexts. *Justice in transition* analyzes how subjects of justice change when objects of justice change—even if subjects of justice are said not to change—and how this can effect categories of collective identification and trigger social transformations beyond given ideas of justice (see chap. 4). *Justice in conflict* highlights that people are usually placed between multiple justice imaginaries that work either together or against each other and attribute different and sometimes contradictory obligations to responsible agents of justice, which need to be weighed against one another (see chap. 5).

The workings of justice and their relation to the collective maintenance of an exploitive old-style plantation economy by tea laborers, trade unionists, and tea planters must be understood within the historical and current transformations of the political economy of tea production in Assam that are discussed in the next section.

Political Economy of Assam Tea in Transition

The Cradle of Industrial Tea

The region of Assam is considered the cradle of industrial tea production and remains the largest tea-cultivating region in India (Mishra et al. 2012, 3–4). As one of India's northeastern federal states, Assam is located between India's international borders with Bhutan, China, Bangladesh, and Myanmar. The only land connection between India's Northeast and other parts of India is the Siliguri Corridor bordered by Bangladesh and Nepal. Sanjib Baruah (2020, 1) describes Northeast India as "an artifact of deliberate policy" because the region was "put together for mundane administrative reasons" (25).

Large parts of Northeast India were ruled by Ahom kings between the thirteenth and nineteenth centuries, and Assam's landscape was dominated by forest areas and small urban clusters with a few thousand inhabitants until the nineteenth century (J. Sharma 2011, 1–2). While Assam's difficult geographical accessibility, due to its hilly landscape and the absence of wheel-ready roads, helped the region to remain politically independent—for instance, from Mughal rulers in Central India—it also led to the perception of Assam as a "remote periphery" (2). The East India Company's military intervention in Assam between 1824 and

1826 to "protect" Assam from Burmese expansionist endeavors, in what is called the first Anglo-Burmese war, resulted in the British annexation of Assam and neighboring chiefdoms (A. Guha 2016, 1). The British annexation of Assam provided the basis for the establishment of commercial tea cultivation in the region (Xaxa 1996, 16–19).

The beginning of the commercial tea cultivation in Assam in the late 1830s coincided with a growing popularity of tea in Britain beyond a small elite circle and a wider circulation among people from a working-class background (Chatterjee 2001, 43). To meet the growing demand, the British first tried to intensify trade with China, where tea was locally cultivated and consumed in monasteries since about the fourth century BCE (Besky 2014, 3). Opium was smuggled illegally to China from India and sold for silver. The silver then could be used to pay for the official tea supply from China. Yet, the growing demand and stricter constrictions on opium trade by China made new strategies necessary to guarantee the tea supply (3–6). These developments can be seen in the context of the beginning of the nineteenth century, when the British gradually started to acquire political functions in India (J. Sharma 2011, 27).

The common narrative about the first tea leaf discovery in Assam tells the story of Charles and Robert Bruce, two brothers and colonial officers who undertook an expedition to the Assam-Burma border in 1823 and discovered native tea plants in the forests of Assam, which were used by the Singpho and Khamti groups for medical and ritual purposes. But "no one ever validated the Bruces' observations, and the 'jungle' tea bushes of Assam remained a myth for several more years" (Besky 2014, 51). It was only a decade later, when an army officer called Andrew Charlton sent tea leaves from Assam to the Tea Committee, that the potential of Assam as a tea-growing region was discovered. The Tea Committee had been established in 1834 by Lord Bentinck, governor-general in India at that time, to look for suitable land to grow tea within India to gain independence from Chinese tea supply (J. Sharma 2011, 29). The first Assam tea, which was sold in London in 1838, was a success. It was auctioned twenty times the price of Chinese tea. This was not, however, because of its taste—which was merely acceptable—but because of the excitement over being able to grow tea in a British colony (31–32). The tea industry was quickly privatized into a single corporation, the Assam Company, which was founded in 1839. However, the "wild" Assam plant was only valued "after its modification by Chinese culture and western science" (31). Chinese tea production served as a model for the establishment of the tea industry in Assam, but planters envisioned the Assam tea industry to become more efficient through mechanization, on the one hand, and better labor organization, on the other hand.

There was a linguistic shift from "tea forest" to "tea garden," which indicated private property as opposed to previously communally owned property, after the Charter Act of 1833 facilitated landownership for Europeans in India and encouraged the British rather than Indians to engage in agrarian enterprises in Assam (34, 40). The Wasteland Rules of 1838 further regulated that people could apply for long-term leases of land if they had a particular amount of capital. This did not explicitly exclude Indians but excluded them indirectly because hardly any Indian had the amount of capital required for leasing land. Applicants for long-term leases of land could then get land cheaply (34–35). Many lands granted for tea remained uncultivated for some time, which guaranteed the British tenants free access to timber and other natural resources that were communally owned previously (40). In addition, tax was much lower or freehold for plantation owners and high for local cultivators (85). Due to these legal incentives, which were guaranteed, early British tea planters faced no scarcity of land and capital at the time when the tea industry was established in Assam, yet the availability of labor turned out to be difficult for them.

In the beginning of industrial tea production in India, laborers were recruited from China, but Chinese laborers were unwilling to do hard manual labor and were comparatively expensive. Therefore, the British looked for an alternative cheap and hardworking labor force from the mid-nineteenth century onward (40). First, they considered local inhabitants of Assam, who were either rice-cultivating subsistence farmers in the Brahmaputra plains or nomads in the hilly regions of Assam. They, however, did not agree to work on long-term contracts; tea labor was not appealing because wages were low, and work was hard on the plantations (38–39). In 1885, the Indian Tea Association was founded to solve the so-called labor question.

A decision was made to recruit laborers mainly from the eastern part of the "tribal belt" in North India, also called the Chotanagpur Plateau, which includes (parts of) the present-day states of Chhattisgarh, Odisha, Jharkhand, and Bihar in central and eastern North India. This is a hot, dry, famine-ridden region and has the highest number of Indigenous populations in India. According to Indian census data (of 1911 and 1921), 50–60 percent of the recruited labor force were Adivasis (called "tribals" or "aboriginals" in the census), around 30 percent came from lower castes, and about 10–15 percent were categorized as caste Hindus (Behal 2014, 255–256).[17] Laborers from the Chotanagpur area were also recruited to other regions and fields of labor. They worked, for example, as indentured laborers on plantations overseas. After slavery was legally abolished in India in 1843, the migrant laborers on tea plantations in Assam were employed as indentured laborers (J. Sharma 2011, 49).[18] Whole families were recruited and employed by distributing tasks along gender and age lines (75). From the beginning of industrial tea production in Assam, the tea industry has employed a relatively high number of women workers compared to other industries in India.

Women work primarily as tea pluckers. Men work mainly, but not exclusively, as field staff or in the factory. Some men also pluck tea. During the colonial era, supervisors were Assamese or Bengali caste Hindus. At the top of the labor hierarchy were British planters (76).[19] Nowadays, some former male (and very few female) tea laborers have become supervisors. Managers today are mainly male Assamese, Bengali, or Marvari caste Hindus.[20]

The "Old-Style" Plantation Economy

The indentured labor system was officially repealed at the beginning of the twentieth century, and after Indian independence, the Plantations Labour Act (PLA) became the most important legal framework that has regulated labor conditions for tea plantation workers in Assam since it was enforced in 1951; it applies to all plantations in India.[21] The PLA makes provisions for working hours, paid and unpaid holidays, wages, and health and welfare facilities, as well as control and punishment mechanisms for violations against the act. The regular working hours are forty-eight hours per week. Workers work from Monday to Saturday. According to the act, no worker shall be allowed to work for more than nine hours per day or fifty-four hours per week. Overtime work must be paid at twice the rate of the ordinary wages. In addition to public holidays, the workers are entitled to one day of rest (unpaid) every week and a day of leave with wages for every twenty working days. Sick leave is guaranteed if laborers provide a proper medical certificate. Women are, moreover, entitled to (prenatal and postnatal) maternal leave. According to the act, every worker must be informed about these regulations by the plantations' management. The PLA prescribes drinking water supply, accessible latrines and urinals, and medical facilities for all workers. Educational and housing facilities shall also be provided as well as canteens and crèches. All nonmonetary benefits shall be provided for workers and their family members alike. As per PLA, public access must be guaranteed "to those parts of the plantation wherein the workers are housed" (Section 16f). The 2010 amendment also prescribes safety provisions for workers dealing with insecticides, chemicals, and toxic substances (Chapter IV A). The state government appoints inspectors who can visit plantations at any time to examine whether the provisions are followed by the plantations' management. If the provisions and regulations are violated, the offender is to be punished with imprisonment (up to six months) and may be fined (up to ten thousand rupees). Any further violation by the same person is to be punished with up to one-year imprisonment and/or a monetary fine.

Laborers receive part of their payment in cash and part of it in kind following a dual wage structure. For the definition of wages, the PLA refers to the Minimum Wages Act (Section 2 [h]). The section defines wages as "all remuneration, capable of being expressed in terms of money." Wage increases used to be negotiated bilaterally between the trade union for tea plantation laborers, the Assam Chah Mazdoor Sangha (ACMS), and the tea planters' Consultative Committee of Plantation Associations (CCPA) in the Assam Valley. Wage agreements are supposed to be revised every three years (Mishra et al. 2012, 105).[22] The 15th Indian Labour Conference of 1957 decided on a need-based minimum wage that calculates three units of consumption (two adults and two children) per wage of a worker. However, the tea planters protested this calculation by arguing that every family on a plantation has at least two workers since employment is family based. Therefore, only one and a half units of consumption should be considered for determining workers' wages. The Central Wage Board for the Tea Plantation Industry declared the planters' argument baseless, but the planters "obstinately stuck to their own concept of wage determination. As a result, tea plantation workers are the lowest paid in the organised sector" (Bhowmik et al. 1996, 9).

Wages are fixed on a timely basis for a whole working day. Moreover, tea pluckers must pluck a minimum of tea leaves (currently twenty-four kilos) to receive their full wage and get incentives for plucking beyond prescribed kilos. Wages in North India are much lower than in South India, but North Indian plantations provide more benefits in-kind for workers. However, the wages in the north are still lower than in the south even after including all nonmonetary benefits (Mishra et al. 2012, 108–109). The Equal Remuneration Act of 1975 declared that equal wages had to be paid for male and female workers. Assam implemented the equal remuneration only in 1990, while other states introduced it much earlier, such as West Bengal, who implemented equal wages in 1976 (Xaxa 1996, 24).

Since the wage negotiations in 2014/2015, the Assam government has advised the wage negotiations with a Minimum Wage Advisory Committee. Until 2014, tea plantation laborers' wages in the Assam Valley were increased by just a few rupees per year, after which the increases became bigger: From Rs. 94 in 2014, they jumped to Rs. 115 in 2015; to Rs. 126 in 2016; to Rs. 137 in 2017; to Rs. 205 in 2021; to Rs. 232 in 2022, and to currently Rs. 250 since 2023.

The PLA has been criticized mainly for its lack of implementation (Banerji and Willoughby 2019; Rowlatt and Deith 2015) and for its creation of laborers' dependence on plantation welfare provisions. Therefore, the labor law regime based on the PLA has been described "as a form of bondage" (Besky 2017a, 619) or "modern-day slavery" (Ray 2016). Tea plantations have been called "states within states" (Raman 2015, 146), and tea companies have been said to "act as a welfare state" (Raj 2013, 477), due to the encompassing welfare measures of the PLA.

Current Transformations in the Political Economy of Assam Tea

The "old-style" political economy of Assam tea production based on regulations of the Plantations Labour Act is currently transforming. Transformations started to develop from the 1970s onward. After India required foreign capital to be "Indianized" in the Foreign Exchange Regulation Act (FERA) of 1973, international companies withdrew from Indian tea production. This process had already started with Indian independence, when British companies turned to other tea-growing regions among its colonies, such as Kenya (Raman 2015, 148). India was the largest tea exporter until the 1960s but is now only the fourth-largest exporter (Mishra et al. 2012, 35–36) after Kenya, China, and Sri Lanka (Tea Board of India 2017, 10).[23] Accordingly, one factor that is said to have caused the "plantation crisis" (Raj 2022), which lasted from about 1998 to 2008, was an oversupply of tea in the world market causing falling sales prices of tea. India had higher production costs than, for example, Kenya or Sri Lanka. A tariffication and regional free trade among countries of the South Asian Association for Regional Cooperation, additionally, increased India's imports of low-quality tea from other Asian countries, such as Sri Lanka or Bangladesh (Raman 2015, 151). The tea crisis is also said to be caused by a decrease in the productivity of tea bushes due to poor management and maintenance of plantations. Last, the disintegration of the Soviet Union is often seen as a main factor that contributed to the crisis because it was the main importer of Indian tea (Raj 2013, 471). While global exports of Indian tea have decreased significantly during the crisis, domestic tea consumption has increased at lower prices (Raman 2015, 152). During the Indian tea crisis, 118 tea estates were closed in India between 2000 and 2005 (158). The closures have affected seventy thousand tea workers. On some closed plantations, cases of starvation and suicides were reported, while on other plantations, workers organized themselves to keep the tea production running, sometimes with help from trade unions (Raman 2015, 158–160). Tea plantation closures were less in Assam than in other tea-growing regions in India (Mishra et al. 2012, 15). Statistics from the Tea Board of India suggest that Indian tea markets recovered from the crisis by the end of 2010 (see Raj 2013, 480).[24]

Multinational companies started to withdraw from tea production on large-scale plantations in Assam during the crisis. The Foreign Exchange Management Act (FEMA) of 2000 again liberalized trade in India and "in the wake of the post-1990s neo-liberalisation, the Government of India permitted a 100 percent FDI [Foreign Direct Investment] in tea in a throwback to the colonial era" (Raman 2015, 149). However, international companies lost interest in Indian tea production. Tea plantations are either owned by the government or by private companies. Private companies are either "vertically integrated tea manufacturers with a stake in all the nodes along the entire value chain . . . whose operations span plantations, trading and blending" or local companies "with stakes in certain nodes alone . . . in the lower segments of the value chain" (Raman 2015, 151). Hindustan Unilever used to be the largest integrated tea manufacturer in India and Assam, followed by Tata Consumer Products Limited. Both companies withdrew from the production of tea in the mid-2000s and started to focus solely on packaging, branding, and marketing tea, which constitute the more profitable elements of the tea sector (Columbia Law School 2014, 16). While Hindustan Unilever sold all its plantations (mainly to McLeod Russel), Tata reached out to the International Finance Corporation to establish a new company called Amalgamated Plantations Private Limited (APPL), which took over Tata's tea plantations and therefore its production by implementing shared ownership and diversifying beyond tea (Columbia Law School 2014, 7).

During this time, the number of small tea growers increased. The state of Assam has approximately 803 tea plantations, which employ altogether 686,000 laborers, and it is assumed that at least that many or more people live on tea plantations as dependents of the workers (Mishra et al. 2012, 81–82; Raj 2013, 471).[25] However, tea production on plantations made up less than 50 percent of the tea produced in India in 2022 (Tea Board of India 2022). The majority was produced by small growers, who are steadily increasing and thereby changing the political economy of tea production in India. Small growers raise tea on smaller plots of land of about two acres and sell fresh tea leaves to so-called Bought Leaf Factories, where the tea is processed and further sold (K. Das 2012). It is estimated that about five laborers work on a tea smallholding (Borah 2013, 86). Yet, since most small growers are excluded from important labor laws, they do not have to make the same provisions for their laborers, and they mainly offer only temporary employment (Biggs et al. 2018). While Kaberi Borah (2013) and others (e.g., Besky 2017b) consider tea smallholdings a potentially promising opportunity for self-employment of tea laborers or rural population, tea plantation laborers whom I met hardly became smallholders because they did not own sufficient land to start a smallholding but would also never work on a smallholding because the labor conditions are much worse compared to plantation work. The casualization of labor has also increased on large-scale plantations since the 1990s (Mishra et al. 2012, 9).

The political economy of Assam tea production is also shaped by significant changes in the legal framework governing plantation labor in India. The Indian government has consolidated forty-four labor laws in India into four new labor codes, covering wages, industrial relations, social security and welfare, and safety and working conditions. While the implementation of these new labor laws is ongoing, the impact on plantations remains unclear. Proposed changes include the repeal of the Plantations Labour Act and the elimination of the dual wage structure (Singh 2020). The two paragraphs of the Occupational Safety, Health and Working Conditions Code of 2020 on plantations are much less comprehensive and less legally binding as compared to the Plantations Labour Act. For example, section 92 of the new code stipulates that "the State Government *may* prescribe requiring every employer to make provisions in his plantation," (emphasis added) while prescriptions in the PLA were framed as legally binding: "It *shall* be the *duty* of every employer to provide and maintain necessary housing accommodation" (emphasis added).

In short, since the 1970s, the political economy of Assam tea has gradually shifted from a scarcity of labor toward an era of labor surplus; from being the world's largest tea exporter to being gradually disarticulated from the capitalist world economy; from a plantation-dominated industry to a gradual replacement of plantations with small growers; from the standard of permanent labor contracts to a casualization of labor; and from welfare labor laws to a new labor law regime that dismantles labor laws characterized by extensive social welfare measures. These transformations are not unique to Assam tea plantations. Colonially established plantation economies are also repealed or radically transformed in other regions of the world. To give but one example, Andrew C. Willford (2014, 6) conducted research on former Tamil rubber plantation workers in Malaysia at a time when "the old, long-term, community-based model of plantation production that was introduced by British and French companies in colonial Malay has been replaced by a model based primarily on itinerant labor, mechanization, and a subsequent gradual contraction of the plantation economy."

Tea planters, trade unionists, and tea laborers' justice imaginaries are equally attached to normative ideals of the old paternalist economy of tea production with a dual wage structure and part compensation in-kind that had initially been created to develop a totalitarian work environment during the colonial establishment of the tea plantation economy in the mid-nineteenth century. When tea plantation laborers, like Anjali who was introduced in the beginning of the book, nowadays defend nonmonetary entitlements to escape the emerging more fully marketized, casualized, and neoliberal economy of tea production, they enter unlikely alliances with the representatives of capital—the tea planters—because the transformation of the tea economy into a landscape of small-farm, casual-labor tea production has neither a place for "labor lines" nor for managers' bungalows.[26] Both of their labor is on the line. Laborers supported the maintenance of the old paternalist economy of tea production along with trade unionists and tea planters because the justice imaginary based on the old paternalist model of tea production "worked" structure-undermining when placed in the context of a new political economy of Assam tea.

Assam Tea Laborers' Manifold Designations

The terminologies used to describe the social composition of the labor force on tea plantations in Assam needs more explanation and critical discussion. The categories are not to be understood as clear-cut, uncontroversial, and fixed. Scholars who engage with the historical development of social categories in India have questioned categories like "Adivasi," "Hindu," or "Dalit" because they are seen as social constructions that were established through administrative practices of British colonial rulers, such as census surveys (see Bates and Shah 2014). A strict social-constructivist perception of these categories, however, has equally been questioned because it is unlikely that the categories emerged from a social vacuum. Categories, at least to a certain extent, resemble then-present social structures although the categories were established and fixed by practices such as the British's meticulous census surveys that later made it difficult to switch between categories or identify situationally with different categories (Eckert 2002, 25).

While it is crucial to reflect on the deconstruction of collective categories, it is also necessary to acknowledge that these categories matter to people and their life worlds in India today. They constitute a social reality for many people. To refer to my field of study, ethnic and religious belonging, for example, played a decisive role with regard to marriage alliances on tea plantations in Assam. There are, nonetheless, limitations to fitting social realities into categories, and, moreover, there is a strategic situational use of these categories, which illustrates that categories as well as their defense or denial are often politically charged. This will be discussed in more detail in chapter 4 (see also Baruah 1986, 1999).

Adivasis constitute the largest group among tea laborers on plantations in Assam, which is different from other tea-growing areas in India where Tamil Dalits (Kerala) or Gorkha (Darjeeling) constitute the majority. The term *Adivasi*, glossed from Hindi, literally means "indigenous," although the indigeneity of Adivasis is controversial in India (see Béteille 1998). The term is used as an umbrella term to designate different ethnic groups, such as Munda or Oraon, which are said to have historically lived mainly in nonsedentary social formations in hilly or forested areas in the so-called tribal belt of Central India. The idea of Adivasi indigeneity in India is based on the Indo-Aryan migration theory, which assumes that Indo-Aryan invaders migrated to North India from Central Asia around 1500 BCE and subjugated the local population. According to the

Indo-Aryan migration theory, the Indo-Aryan invaders are seen as the ancestors of higher-caste Hindus, while the local population, which lived in India at the time of the Indo-Aryan invasion, is seen as indigenous to India—therefore called "Adivasis" (Kulke and Rothermund 1998, 44–46). However, Hindu fundamentalists challenge the Indo-Aryan migration theory by stating that Indo-Aryans were also indigenous to the Indian subcontinent and did not migrate to India from Central Asia. They call Adivasis "Vanvasis" instead, which literally means "forest dwellers," to emphasize that they do not deserve any special "indigenous" status in India. The Indian government also objects Adivasis' claim to indigeneity, arguing that "the entire population of the country at the time of independence from British rule and their successors are indigenous" (Parmar 2016, 6), which makes "indigeneity" obsolete. Instead, the Indian government categorizes Adivasis as Scheduled Tribes (ST). Adivasis are often equated with Scheduled Tribes and vice versa in India. However, the terms have a different trajectory. Scheduled Tribes are those "tribes" listed in the periodically revised schedule of the Indian constitution who have historically been discriminated against and who are officially characterized by their "primitive" traits, distinctive culture, geographical isolation, shyness of contact with the community at large, and overall "backwardness" (Government of India 2005). The Indian Constituent Assembly decided to use the term *Scheduled Tribes* instead of *Adivasis* when it drafted the Indian Constitution against the opinion of the Adivasi representative Jaipal Singh because the term *Adivasi* would lack legal specificity (Parmar 2016, 5–6).[27] Therefore, the term *Adivasi* has limited legal significance in India today (6).

Scheduled Tribes is one of the administrative categories for minorities in India next to Scheduled Castes and Other Backward Classes (OBC). The Bharatiya Janata Party (BJP) government introduced further 10 percent reservations for so-called Economically Weaker Sections (EWS) with the Constitution (124th Amendment) Bill of 2019 (Kumar 2023, 193). More than seven hundred ethnic groups are recognized as Scheduled Tribes in India. They constitute about 8.6 percent of the Indian population, or 104 million people (International Work Group for Indigenous Affairs 2021, 205). People categorized as ST are eligible to affirmative action by the Indian government to facilitate social upward mobility through preferences in public sector jobs and educational institutions and in the electoral sphere (Deshpande 2013, 56). It is the different federal states that recommend to the union government which ethnic groups are acknowledged as Scheduled Tribes. This means that some ethnic groups that are categorized as ST in one Indian federal state are not necessarily recognized as such in another state. The ethnic groups (e.g., Munda, Oraon, Saora) that are designated as Adivasis and acknowledged as Scheduled Tribes in Central Indian states such as Chhattisgarh, Odisha, Jharkhand, and Bihar are not among the twenty-nine ethnic groups that are acknowledged as Scheduled Tribes in Assam (Ministry of Tribal Affairs 2019). Adivasis constitute the majority of Assam's tea plantation laborers, who moved to Assam as labor migrants from Central India (A. Sharma and Khan 2018, 196), and in Assam, they are categorized as OBC. The OBC category was introduced in 1980 with the Mandal Commission report and was implemented in the 1990s. It considers economic dimensions in addition to historical discrimination based on ethnicity or caste but does not provide the same affirmative action provisions as the Scheduled Tribes category (Deshpande 2013, 52–53).

Tea plantation laborers' shared migration history results in them being labeled as "tea tribes" in postcolonial Assam, and those who migrated to the villages in Assam from the tea plantations are called "ex-tea tribes." According to the labor historian Rana Behal, the category of "tea tribes" came up in the 1920s when managers started to produce data on "tea tribes" for manager trainings. The category has gained official status to some extent, manifested, for instance, in official administrative designations such as the "Tea Tribes and Adivasi Welfare Department" of the Assamese government. Tea plantation laborers are also designated as *bāgāniyā* or *bāgān ke log* (lit. "people of the garden"). The term *bāgān* literally means "garden" in Assamese (and Hindi)—which is a commonly used euphemism for the large-scale capitalist tea plantations in Assam. While still commonly used in Assam, the terms *tea tribes*, *ex-tea tribes*, and *bāgāniyā* are considered highly problematic by Adivasi activists (see chap. 4).

In the following chapters, the situational contingency, political dimension, and strategic appropriation of Assam tea plantation laborers' different (self)designations will demonstrate the flexibility and ambiguity of these terms in practice. In the next section, I will now turn to the background of my empirical research.

"This Is Me Here in the Field . . ."

I conducted altogether thirteen months of fieldwork in India between 2014 and 2017, divided into three research stays. I visited different plantations in the Assam districts of Cachar, Jorhat, Sonitpur, Dibrugarh, and the Bodoland Territorial Region. Initially, I commuted between Delhi and Assam to follow different activists working for tea laborers in Assam when I was a research affiliate at the Centre for the Study of Law and Governance at the Jawaharlal Nehru University in Delhi. While I conducted semistructured and informal interviews with representatives of all interest groups that represented tea laborers, I spent most of my time together with Adivasi activists and the international nongovernment organization (NGO) representatives who guided them. I conducted participant observation at legal capacity trainings, protests, and activists' meetings. Moreover, I stayed in an NGO training center for some time, which was located next to a government-owned plantation with about two thousand permanent laborers. During my fieldwork, I lived for altogether six months in a "labor line" (labor quarter) on a privately owned plantation in Lower Assam, which I call Dolani Tea Estate, with around fifteen hundred permanent laborers. While I stayed on Dolani Tea Estate, I was able to participate and observe many aspects of the laborers' daily lives: I went to work with tea pluckers and plucked tea with them, I hung out with laborers in their spare time in the afternoon and evening, I took part in celebrations, and so forth. In 2015, I also stayed in a manager's bungalow on a plantation in Jorhat district. In addition to participant observation among activists, laborers, and managers, I visited tea auction houses in Guwahati and Kolkata to get some insights into the selling and distribution of Assam tea (see chap. 5). I conducted problem-centered qualitative interviews with representatives from tea research institutions, such as the Tocklai Tea Research Institute and the Agricultural University in Jorhat city. Altogether, I conducted seventy-four interviews with tea plantation workers, their children, staff members, former tea workers, managers, owners, activists, trade unionists, tea brokers, and researchers, in either English, Hindi, or Sadri. While I speak English and Hindi fluently, the plantation laborers mainly spoke their own ethnic groups' languages at home and Sadri as a lingua franca. Sadri is to some extent related to Hindi but not identical, and there were many different Sadri dialects spoken on different plantations. After some time, I was able to understand the Sadri dialect spoken on Dolani Tea Estate well enough to follow ordinary conversations, which made mutual understanding not ideal but possible. However, I conducted interviews in Sadri mainly with the help of formal research assistants or informal translators such as children of laborers who spoke better Hindi than their parents.

At the beginning of my field research, a researcher asked me whether I would like to take part in a study that examined researchers' emotions while conducting empirical research. My participation included, among other things, answering some questions during the research. In a questionnaire that I answered in 2015, one of these questions was to complete the sentence "This is me here in the field." I wrote, "I am the tall, white woman who wears Indian clothes, works with the workers, sits with them on the floor to eat rice with her hands, who speaks Hindi fluently, and who somehow fits in here surprisingly well, and yet is still a stranger." Debarati Sen (2017, 35) describes herself as "insider-outsider" in her field of study with Nepali tea workers in Darjeeling. She is an insider because she is an Indian woman speaking Nepali fluently. But she remains an outsider as a middle-class and upper-caste *bhadramohila* "deeply aware of my class and caste privilege in India" (40). I was an "insider-outsider" in a different way. What helped me to "somehow fit in here surprisingly well" was that I had already lived and worked in India with marginalized people for some time before conducting my research on Assam tea plantations. What probably also helped me to fit in was that I come from a working-class family in rural Germany. Therefore, conversation patterns with the tea laborers were more "habitual" (Bourdieu 1977) for me than conversations with upper-class academics are for me to date. However, as a foreigner, I remained an obvious stranger from a globally seen structurally privileged position compared to tea workers, activists, and managers alike.

Chapter Outline

In the introduction I suggest that justice—what people consider to be due to them and others—is inevitably "at work," which means that justice imaginaries maintain, enhance, or limit people's odds to act and vice versa. Based on this premise, each chapter of this book elaborates different workings of justice.

The first chapter analyzes how justice imaginaries work on different scales. I show how a "methodological enclavism" in plantation studies naturalized an analytical view on plantation labor as immobile, bounded, and fixed. I attempt an epistemic move to create new foci in studies of plantation work that move beyond "methodological enclavism" and reconsider plantations as permeable and transforming spaces and show that certain forms of inequality and injustice attributed to plantation economies due to methodological enclavism need to be located beyond plantation enclaves. I argue that tea labor is not spatially immobile but that spatial mobility does not necessarily lead to upward social mobility. Regarding the workings of justice, chapter 1 illustrates that when defining plantations as the scale to address matters of justice, responsible agents of justice (tea planters) can be more clearly identified as those responsible for implementing labor justice to tea laborers. When upscaling questions of justice beyond plantations, economic exploitation and structural casteism beyond Assam tea plantations can be addressed. However, responsible agents of justice are more difficult to define. Justice works differently on different scales, highlighting certain aspects of justice while disregarding others.

Chapters 2 and 3 analyze justice in context. The second chapter introduces life and work on Assam tea plantations in ethnographic fiction. I composed different observations of my fieldwork into one fictive day on a plantation through the eyes of Jiya, a tea laborer on Dolani Tea Estate. The narrative introduces differently positioned actors on Assam tea plantations and hints at their everyday conceptualizations of justice. Tea laborers demonstrate loyalty toward tea companies, which is part of laborers' justice imaginaries, further elaborated in chapter 3. Based on the argument by James Scott (1976, 158) that injustice can only be perceived if people have a norm of justice in mind from which it has departed, chapter 3 explores tea plantation laborers' open and hidden protests in order to understand underlying norms of justice. I argue that many laborers aspired to be acknowledged for their hard work and rather held onto effectuating the "old" political economy of tea production based on regulations of the Plantations Labour Act. Justice in context suggests that when justice imaginaries are placed into another context, they can turn from structure-preserving frames of justice into structure-undermining frames of justice. Justice ideals of the "old" political economy of tea production that worked structure-preserving in the twentieth century, turn into structure-undermining frames of justice when placed in the context of a new political economy of tea production in the twenty-first century.

Chapter 4 focuses on how changing concepts of justice in organized labor struggles transform tea laborers' categories of collective identification and leadership patterns among labor rights activists working on behalf of Assam tea laborers. While activists as concerned agents of justice claim to embrace better objects of justice, such as affirmative action or minimum wages, in order to give seemingly identical subjects of justice (tea workers, Adivasis, subjects of labor rights) what is due to them, the scope of the categories of collective identification of subjects of justice are adapted situationally flexible, which also impacts who is seen as the concerned agents of justice.

Chapter 5 analyzes justice in conflict, taking tea planters' "bungalow doctrines" as an example. Tea planters' gestures of proximity have been interpreted in the literature on tea plantations as a means to exploit rather than being truly affectionate toward laborers. I analyze planters' structural position in the tea plantation economy between different justice imaginaries that make different, contradictory claims on them. I argue that different justice imaginaries work together or against one another when people try to balance the different demands posed on them by different justice imaginaries.

While the analysis of the workings of justice was deducted from my experience of living and working with different actors on Assam tea plantations when dealing with the puzzling observation of unexpected alliances, I suggest that *justice at work* can be operationalized in other settings, including in other Indian contexts and beyond.[28] In the conclusion, I discuss empirical examples that are not related to Assam tea plantations, in which the analytical lens of different workings of justice may be applied to demonstrate the more general analytical value of *justice at work*. The concluding chapter also draws more general political conclusions. I content to resist the low-hanging fruit of fundamentally critiquing the tea plantation economy when there is labor on the line.

1

SCALES OF JUSTICE WITHIN AND BEYOND PLANTATION "ENCLAVES"

Raju was in his mid-forties when I met him in October 2015. He came to Dolani Tea Estate together with his parents from the Central Indian state of Odisha when he was three years old. Raju now had three children of his own. When I visited Raju's family, he was frustrated about his work and life on the plantation. He complained about the hardship of labor, but most of all, he was upset about how caste hierarchies were blurred on the plantation:

> They call us Adivasis here, but we are Gwala. We are higher caste (*jāt*) compared to Adivasi.[1] There are only seven other families on this plantation who belong to our caste; the others are lower caste. But people here, they do not believe in purity (*śuddh*) and impurity (*aśuddh*). It does not work here. In Orissa [the former name of the Indian federal state Odisha], people believe in purity and live accordingly. Higher castes and lower castes do not live together like here. I do not like how people live together here, without consideration for purity and impurity.

When I wanted to visit Raju one year later, he and his family had gone back to Odisha. His story is striking in several regards. Raju's story does not fit the common narrative that tea plantation laborers were recruited from Central India by British planters as indentured laborers during the colonial era and "got stuck" on the plantations for generations in forced immobility (see, e.g., AK 2015; Banerji and Willoughby 2019; Columbia Law School 2014, 25–26; Lahiri 2000; Nagar and Feruglio 2016; A. Sharma and Khan 2018, 187).

By presenting tea plantation laborers' oral histories, such as Raju's, in this chapter I illustrate how ongoing postcolonial labor migration to and from Assam tea plantations challenges the image of unchanged and isolated tea plantation enclaves. I argue that Assam tea plantations are permeable and transforming spaces with mobile inhabitants. This reconceptualization of plantation spaces draws attention to how certain injustices, such as economic precarity or caste stigmatization, that have been attributed to plantation economies exist, even more so, beyond the plantation enclaves (see also Raj 2022). Adapting the argument by Nancy Fraser (2010) that the "Westphalian" nation-state is not appropriate to discuss matters of justice in a globalized world, this chapter questions the imagined plantation "enclaves" as appropriate "scales of justice" and thereby contributes to more general considerations about how justice works on different scales. I argue that imagining justice within plantation enclaves enables concerned agents of justice to address clearly identifiable responsible agents of justice past (British planters) and present (Indian tea planters) for their success or failure to give their subjects of justice (tea plantation laborers) what is due to them (labor justice). However, upscaling concerns about justice beyond plantation enclaves allows concerned agents of justice to address injustice beyond tea plantations even though responsible agents of justice are less clearly identifiable and therefore less easily addressable.

The first part of the chapter introduces the characteristics of the indentured labor regime, under which plantations were regulated in the nineteenth and early twentieth centuries, and discusses how the establishment of industrial tea production on plantations in Assam was dependent on migrant laborers from Central India. Based on laborers' oral histories, the second section of this chapter demonstrates that labor migration to plantations in Assam did not stop with Indian independence, as suggested in common narratives of Assam tea plantation laborers' intergenerational immobility. Labor migration continued into the second half of the twentieth century. Further relativizing the image of immobility and enclosure, the third part analyzes why tea laborers decide to leave plantation work in postcolonial India and under what circumstances spatial mobility leads to upward social mobility. In the final section, I suggest conceptualizing tea plantations as transforming and permeable spaces instead of as enclaves and discuss how justice works within and beyond plantations.

Understanding plantations as permeable spaces draws attention to the facts that (1) laborers continue to migrate to Assam tea plantations in postcolonial India; (2) plantations are permeable on an everyday level because they constitute a refuge for workers' dependents, who engage in other activities outside the plantations, since only about 33 percent of those living on tea plantations in Assam are permanent laborers (Mishra et al. 2012, 115); (3) some laborers quit their jobs and engage in other activities outside the plantation economy; and, most importantly, (4) injustices exist beyond plantation enclaves, and laborers who do not belong to a higher caste, like Raju, do not necessarily experience upward social mobility even if they move out of the plantations.

The Indentured Labor Regime

The industrial production of tea on Assam tea plantations was initiated by British planters under colonial rule in India in the late 1830s, as described in the introduction. After attempts to recruit laborers from China and locals from Assam failed and the lack of laborers to establish the tea industry became a severe problem for the first tea planters, the Indian Tea Association was founded in 1885 to solve the so-called labor question, which meant finding ways to regulate labor recruitment for tea planters in Assam. It was decided to recruit laborers mainly from the eastern part of the "tribal belt" in North India or Chotanagpur Plateau. It has been argued that the erosion of Adivasis' communal property rights over land, water, and forest by the colonial government helped to force people from Central India to migrate to Assam (Mishra et al. 2012, 98). Since slavery was legally abolished in India in 1843, the migrant laborers on tea plantations in Assam were employed not as slaves but as indentured laborers (J. Sharma 2011, 49). It is, however, controversially debated, among historians in general and among labor historians working on tea plantations in Assam in particular, whether indentured labor was different from slavery in type or degree or, in other words, whether indentured labor was rather a "new kind of slavery" (Varma 2016, 2–3; see also Behal and Mohapatra 1992, 142–144).

The indentured labor system was introduced on plantations in Assam through two legislations: the Workmen's Breach of Contract Act XIII of 1859 and the Act VI of the Bengal Council of 1865 (Behal and Mohapatra 1992). What both acts had in common was that they provided tea planters with the right to exert penal provisions on their laborers if they were held responsible for any breach of contract. The second act applied only to newly recruited laborers and not to formerly recruited time-expired or locally recruited laborers. It scheduled contracts to a minimum term of three years; prescribed a monthly minimum wage (Rs. 5 for men and Rs. 4 for women), daily working time (nine hours), and a government inspector to examine the proper implementation of the act; and it enabled planters to sanction laborers when they violated their contracts. Sanctions included imprisonment without warrant and private arrest on plantations (Behal and Mohapatra 1992, 146). The first act, which was extended to Assam in 1864, applied only to locally recruited laborers, such as Kachari. It gave planters fewer comprehensive rights than the penal contract system of the second act—for example, no right to private arrest (147).

The recruitment of tea plantation laborers under the indentured labor regime from the Chotanagpur Plateau was conducted either through private contractors or sirdars. Sirdars, also called sardars, were former plantation laborers who upgraded to become overseers or supervisors. They were sent out by their managers to recruit in their home districts (Behal 2014, 256). Labor recruitment was either unregistered (i.e., recruitment by unlicensed contractors) or registered. Unregistered recruitment gradually became the norm rather than the exception (Behal and Mohapatra 1992, 151). It was structured into different levels of recruitment and accordingly caused high costs for planters due to different levels of middlemen who tried to earn as much profit as possible per laborer they recruited (152). Labor recruitment was wavelike rather than constant. The reasons for recruitment peaks included harvest losses and starvation in the recruiting areas or increased demand for tea worldwide, as well as a recurring necessity for fresh labor due to higher mortality rates than birth rates among laborers because of malnourishment, epidemics, frequent abortions, ex–tea laborers' migration to the countryside in Assam to settle as tenant cultivators after their indentured contracts ended, and large extensions of tea acreage (Behal 2014, 254–255). Whole families were recruited and employed by distributing tasks along gender and age lines (J. Sharma 2011, 75). The recruited tea plantation laborers, also called "coolies," were at the bottom of the labor hierarchies.[2] Above them were supervisors who were Assamese or Bengali caste Hindus, and at the top of the labor hierarchy were British planters (76).

The penal contract system under the indentured labor law was gradually dismantled when planters' power of private arrest was withdrawn and unlicensed recruitment completely abolished in 1908. With the abolition of the Workmen's Breach of Contract Act in 1926, the last piece of the indentured labor system was legally dismantled (Behal and Mohapatra 1992, 167) and tea plantations in Assam became regulated under the Plantations Labour Act of 1951, which no longer legally forced laborers to stay on plantations for an agreed period of time and did not give planters the legal right to enforce penal sanctions on laborers who broke their labor contracts.

Narratives Beyond the Long-Bygone Migration

The common narrative about Assam's tea plantation laborers is that they were recruited from Central India by British planters during the colonial era as indentured laborers and have remained on the plantations for generations in forced immobility until today. I had taken this narrative for granted until two permanent tea pluckers on Dolani Tea Estate, Elisabeth and her husband, Manoj, invited me to visit them in their home in 2015. During our conversation, Elisabeth sent her daughter to the kitchen to make tea for us and then she disappeared into the next room for a moment. She came back holding a document showing that her father had migrated to Assam in 1966 when he was thirty-two years old. This was the first time a tea plantation laborer had told me a personal postcolonial migration story. I thought Elisabeth's story must be exceptional.

I had taken the narrative of a long-bygone migration for granted because it was relayed to me during many conversations about Assam's tea plantation laborers by people from outside the plantations during my early stages of fieldwork. Additionally, this narrative is undergirded by scholarly and activist studies of Assam's tea plantations. One article states that "almost the majority of the workforce of the tea plantations . . . were brought to Assam as indentured laborers by British planters more than 120 years ago" (AK 2015). Another study claims, "These Adivasis are the descendants of the workers who were brought by the British from the Chota Nagpur Plateau to work in the tea plantations of Assam three to four generations ago" (A. Sharma and Khan 2018, 187). Another report asserts, "The workers, who were initially migrants, lost contact with their communities of origin while remaining isolated within their new locations. Though active recruitment of new workers stopped in the 1950s, workers continued to live much as they did on arrival, entirely dependent on the plantation" (Columbia Law School 2014, 25–26).

However, during my fieldwork I came across increasing evidence of laborers with migration trajectories to and from Assam's plantations in postcolonial India, such as that of Binod. He had migrated to Assam in the 1970s with his family when he was twelve years old. His family owned a piece of land in Jharkhand and had engaged in subsistence farming before migrating to Assam. He recalled that his family's life in Jharkhand had been fine as long as their harvest was good. But when it did not rain for several seasons in a row, the family's whole crop was spoiled. Binod explained to me that his parents had great difficulty feeding the family during that time. "The situation was so bad that we were not able to eat more than twice a week," he said. "We almost died of thirst and hunger." His family knew people from the neighborhood who had gone to Assam to work on tea plantations. Plantations used to send sardars to the area in big cars to recruit new laborers. Binod told me that rumors had spread in his neighborhood that laborers would be eligible for housing, food rations, and other facilities for free on plantations in Assam. So Binod's family members decided to pack their bare necessities and leave their relatives and piece of land behind to accompany a sardar to Assam.

Many laborers told me that they had come to Assam by themselves or with their parents when they were younger, like Binod. Often, they had owned a piece of land that they had farmed. When their farming could no longer support their livelihood, due to difficult environmental challenges such as droughts or plagues of insects, they suffered severe hunger. Attracted by the promise of a secure livelihood on tea plantations, they decided to migrate to Assam.

These oral narratives of tea plantation laborers' migration histories show that, after the end of the colonial era and the indentured labor system, similar economic precarities impelled people from similar regions and social backgrounds to leave their homes and seek a secure existence on Assam's tea plantations, even though they were no longer legally bound to plantation labor through indentured labor contracts.

The fact that tea plantations came to symbolize minimum economic security due to legally governed welfare measures for labor migrants who were suffering economic deprivation must be contextualized by looking beyond the plantation setting to the precarious nature of farming in India.[3] A study of agricultural labor in Bihar (Kantor 2020) reveals that rural people who grow their own food (and often choose not to call themselves "farmers") are usually unable to cover their household expenses from farming alone. Instead, they rely on "off-farm employment in order to meet rising household expenses" (99). This is also underlined by a growing number of rural Indigenous northeast Indian migrants who seek jobs in Indian metropolitan cities (see Kikon and Karlsson 2019). These studies emphasize that people in rural India are unable to live from farming alone, especially because the agrarian crisis in India has been exacerbated since the 1970s (see Reddy and Mishra 2012), culminating in high suicide rates among farmers in India, especially since the 1990s (Kannuri and Jadhav 2021).

Yet what was striking to me, besides the fact that laborers continued to migrate to Assam's tea plantations after independence, was that laborers did not seem to have migrated in large numbers from Central India to Assam's plantations after the late 1970s. One possible explanation for this may be the gradual "disarticulation" (Bair and Werner 2011) of Assam tea production from the capitalist world market following the economic tea crisis in India (see introduction). This disarticulation was expressed in the withdrawal of global vertically integrated companies like Hindustan Unilever and Tata from tea production in the early 2000s. With the withdrawal of international companies, the ongoing replacement of large-scale plantations with small growers and the casualization of labor has intensified, since tea production no longer constitutes a profitable endeavor. Thus, labor migration to Assam's tea plantations has probably decreased significantly since the 1970s, not because plantation labor is no longer appealing to people living in precarious circumstances off the plantation but because tea companies no longer regularly offer new permanent labor contracts.

Postcolonial Migration

The historical study of the political economy of Assam tea by Rana Behal (2014, 254–255) demonstrates that labor migration away from tea plantations has occurred since colonial times, when laborers migrated to the countryside in Assam to settle as tenant cultivators after their indentured contracts ended. This is evident in the common (and controversial) use of the term *ex–tea tribes* to designate former tea plantation laborers who had migrated to the outskirts of the plantations in Assam.

During my fieldwork, I came across three main types of spatial mobility away from Assam's tea plantations that tea laborers or their children embraced: (1) laborers migrated to the surrounding villages or to laborers' rural home places in Central India to engage in farming; (2) laborers' children migrated temporarily to India's metropolitan cities to work as domestic laborers or factory workers; and (3) laborers' children went away to study and eventually engage in trade union or human rights activism.

Regarding labor migration to villages surrounding the plantations, Manoj's story is telling. Once he confided in me that he was planning to leave the plantation and had already bought a piece of land close to the plantation to engage in subsistence farming. Manoj also complained about plantation work. "It is as if they've tied us up with a big rope," he said. "If we do not work, it is bad, and if we work, it is also bad. . . . As long as we work everything is all right, but the moment we stop working, we do not have anything, neither a house nor food rations." Manoj's purchase of land was his attempt to escape from dependence on the plantation: "By buying land . . . half of my sufferings are gone." When I asked him what the other half of his suffering was about, he answered, "Working for the plantation." Therefore, Manoj planned to leave the plantation once and for all, together with his family. Like Manoj, many other laborers described life and work on tea plantations as *kaṣṭ*—the term for suffering in both Hindi and Sadri—often related to the hardship of plantation labor.[4]

Migration to the outskirts of plantations was also evident in the stories of temporary laborers living off the plantation. Hanisha, for instance, was working as a temporary sardarin (female overseer) on Dolani Tea Estate when I met her in 2015. She lived with her family on the plantation outskirts. She told me that, after her father had died, her mother could no longer afford to pay her school fees and quickly arranged her marriage to a farmer living off the plantation. In October 2015, I sat with Hanisha and some of her relatives, who were all temporary laborers, and learned that all their parents had been permanent laborers on Dolani Tea Estate. When I asked them about their own labor situations, they complained about being employed as just temporary laborers. Although they were getting the same pay as permanent laborers, because the regional wage agreement for tea plantation laborers in Assam is binding for permanent and temporary laborers alike, temporary laborers nevertheless received fewer nonmonetary benefits and were only employed for seven to ten months of the year. One retired woman lamented that laborers had easily obtained permanent positions in previous days, whereas it was exceedingly difficult to get a permanent contract now.

When I asked these temporary laborers what a better life would look like for them, what they aspired to, the women replied that they wanted food rations for their families like the permanent workers, a house on the plantation like permanent workers, and so forth. When I met temporary laborers who lived off the plantation in surrounding villages, they would ask me if I could help them gain a permanent contract on a plantation. Most parents of temporary workers had earlier been permanent workers on a tea plantation and had bought land in the villages around the plantation (often using funds from their retirement scheme) to engage in subsistence farming, but they failed to make a living from farming. Sooner or later, they had to send one or more family members back to work on a plantation. However, by then companies were only giving temporary contracts, so these family members became employed under worse labor conditions than their parents.

Other laborers had migrated to their home regions in Central India to conduct farming. In 2016, I accompanied Vijay, an Adivasi tea laborer who was returning with his family, to Chhattisgarh by train for part of the journey. I had become acquainted with Vijay while I was staying on Dolani Tea Estate. Vijay's father had come to Assam in 1975 in his early twenties and had worked on Dolani Tea Estate until his retirement. Using funds from his retirement scheme, he had bought a piece of land in Chhattisgarh, where he was born.[5] Vijay and his family left the plantation to stay with his father and engage in farming in Chhattisgarh. He had to give up his permanent position on the plantation to do this. I later learned that his father had died in 2019, and Vijay was unable to make a living for his family from farming. He and his wife engaged in temporary wage labor alongside their farming activities to make ends meet. They regretted their decision to leave plantation labor, since their precarious life off the plantation eventually turned out to be more difficult for them than life on the plantation, but they could not gain a permanent position on the plantation again. In the neoliberalized political economy of Assam tea production, where permanent labor contracts are hardly available anymore, this kind of spatial mobility often turned into downward social mobility.

The second common form of mobility, which mainly younger people engaged in, was temporary migration to one of India's metropolitan cities. Young women most often worked as domestic helpers and young men primarily as factory workers. On the plantations where I conducted research, almost every family had a member who had embraced this kind of mobility at some point in life. NGOs framed young people's migration to metropolitan cities as "kidnapping" or "human trafficking" because agents recruited young people from the plantations, often without informing their parents. Sometimes these people were not paid well, or even not at all if they ended up in the wrong location, and some even disappeared completely, which was traumatic for their families. Human rights activists on Dolani Tea Estate had started a theater performance campaign against human trafficking to communicate its dangers to young people. Yet, people who did migrate to a city for domestic or factory work had quite different attitudes toward this type of mobility, based on their own experiences. I met several people who viewed it as a good opportunity to see something new and earn some extra income for the family, since pay there was much higher than the average wages on plantations. One laborer I spoke to reveled in her past as a domestic worker in Delhi:

> In 2007, I once went to Delhi with an agent. The agent arranged every-thing for me. I went for one year. I earned 1,200 rupees per month. Today people earn at least 3,000 rupees. I really loved it. The agent was all right, and my boss as well. One time, they even took me to a five-star restaurant. One meal cost 600 rupees. It was so good. I am immediately ready to go out again, but I am old now and my husband is ill, so I can't go anymore, and nobody would be willing to take me.

Another laborer told me he had sent his daughter to Sikkim when she was four-teen years old. She takes care of two children there, in a family where both par-ents work as teachers. He commented, "My daughter went to a very good family. My daughter really likes how they treat her as if she was their own child." Thus, opinions differ on whether this type of mobility constitutes a dangerous human rights violation or a good opportunity to gain experience and extra income out-side the plantation. This type of mobility is also present in plantations in other parts of India or elsewhere. Mythri Jegathesan (2019, 151–175), for instance, illustrates the nuanced ambiguities and social implications of temporary labor migration to Colombo by children of Hill Country Tamils who work on tea plan-tations in Sri Lanka. Supurna Banerjee (2021) also engages migration decisions of tea plantation workers in Dooars from a feminist perspective. Banerjee argues that mobility and immobility are rather an ever-changing continuum than a fixed opposition when demonstrating how migration can become a form of immobility or fixed entrapment and the desire to end moving can become a marker of social mobility (54). Building on Banerjee's important observations in Dooars, I argue that Assam tea laborers' temporary spatial mobility to cities hardly translated into sustainable socioeconomic upward mobility. I met many laborers who had been to a metropolitan city for a couple of years but eventually returned to Assam to inherit their parents' permanent position on the tea plantation. Thus, while people from tea plantations are not spatially immobile, spatial mobility does not necessarily lead to sustainable upward social mobility.

A third form of mobility that created upward social mobility for a small number of plantation laborers' offspring was engaging in trade union or human rights activism. There were three main interest groups working on behalf of tea plantation laborers in Assam: the regional trade union Assam Chah Mazdoor Sangha; a student association called Assam Tea Tribes Student Association; and a newer social movement of Adivasi activists that includes different organizations working on behalf of tea laborers or Adivasis in Assam in general. I discuss these interest groups in more detail in chapter 4. What is important here, however, is that this third form of labor mobility demonstrates how ethnic and caste affiliations and gender determine whether socioeconomic mobility becomes a corollary of spatial mobility. While Adivasis in Assam used to be excluded from certain affirmative action provisions and from leadership positions in the trade union movement, some male Adivasis were able to gain upward socioeconomic mobility by participating in the Adivasi movement in Assam.

Plantations as Permeable and Transforming Spaces

Like others (e.g., D. Sen 2017) who contested the idea of plantation "enclaves" by pointing to the embeddedness of plantations in the larger sociopolitical and economic locality, the demonstrated widespread migration to and from tea plantations in Assam questions the widespread enclave perspective on plantations that has treated labor mobility as exceptional. Deepak K. Mishra, Vandana Upadhyay, and Atul Sarma, for instance, conducted a quantitative survey on employment and occupational mobility among tea plantation laborers in three districts in Upper Assam (Mishra et al. 2012), concluding that "there seems to be a considerable degree of 'crowding in' of tea garden workers and their families in the tea sector itself. In the context of rapid and increasing mobility of workers across sectors and spaces . . . the apparent intergenerational immobility of tea garden labourers is an important and, to some extent, intriguing question" (2). The authors further state that "invisible chains" would "bind" tea laborers to plantations, without specifying what these are (188). The image of isolation and being unfree is also highlighted in Sharit Bhowmik's work on plantation labor in India. Bhowmik (2011, 250) emphasizes that "despite being a part of the formal sector and having a high degree of unionization, tea plantation workers . . . are not totally free. . . . The result of this situation is that plantations remain enclaves."

Others have described plantation labor as "bonded labor" or "neo-bondage." Souparna Lahiri (2000) argues that "the tea plantation economy in India can . . . be referred to as an enclave economy" because "tea plantation workers of Assam and West Bengal are . . . fourth generation immigrants of indentured migrants from the Central Indian tribal heartland. . . . Generation after generation, they remain tied to the gardens. They are 'born in the gardens and die in the gardens.' They are the epitome of modern-day bonded labour—the forced and unfree labour."

Jayaseelan Raj (2013, 471–479; 2022) studied tea plantation labor in the South Indian state of Kerala, paying attention to how laborers sought alternative means of livelihood during the tea crisis. While highlighting that, during the crisis, "the insular nature of the plantation system breaks up and the workers' engagement with the outside world becomes intense," Raj emphasizes the continued marginalization of plantation laborers in "alienated enclaves" in a form of "neo-bondage." According to Raj (2013, 469–470), "Plantation labour continues to be in an alienated situation that is similar in many ways to that of the indentured system since the historically alienated life situation of the workers is continuously reproduced. . . . The process of alienation . . . is inherent to the plantation system. . . . New forms of alienation . . . operate largely on the foundations laid by the oppressive plantation production processes which emerged under the colonial indenture system."

Sarah Besky (2017a, 619) suggested a theoretical and descriptive tool that she calls "fixity," which "is less a negative correlate to freedom than a multidimensional condition that calls into question the sharp divide between freedom and bondage." This points to the "continued importance of 'fixity' to capitalist regimes of accumulation" (617). While others had highlighted flexibility and mobility as being central to late capitalist agriculture, for Besky, "the 21st-century plantation in India maintains many 'old style' attributes," including "dependence on owners for housing and other facilities as a form of bondage" (619). Therefore, for Besky, the "defining feature" of tea plantations to this day is "an immobile, precarious, fixed labor force" (628). Although some degree of freedom and mobility in plantation labor is acknowledged, the emphasis in the literature remains on bondage, immobility, and fixity.

However, this "enclave perspective," I argue, has limited the view of plantations and plantation labor in India in two ways. First, the enclave perspective has obfuscated the fact that plantations are transforming spaces. The "old-style" plantation, which is said to have remained more or less unchanged, is in fact phasing out, as described in the introduction's section on current transformations in the political economy of tea production. Second, the enclave perspective implies that certain forms of inequality and injustice are characteristic features of plantation economies. This is evident, for instance, in Raj's (2013, 469–470) evaluation that "alienation . . . is inherent to the plantation system" and that "new forms of alienation . . . operate largely on the foundations laid by the oppressive plantation production processes which emerged under the colonial indenture system." This assessment resonates with debates about the Plantationocene.

Donna Haraway et al. (2016) suggested the concept of the "Plantationocene" as an alternative, and more suitable, term to what has become known as the Anthropocene—a point of inflection from the Holocene to a new era (Haraway 2015, 159).[6] The central question posed by the evolving literature on the Plantationocene is how plantation economies have shaped the present, while different key features of plantations (i.e., extraction, extermination, homogenization, inequality, insularity) are foregrounded. The Plantationocene literature has been criticized for not using its potential to analyze racial politics in a meaningful way but rather "obscuring the centrality of racial politics" (Davis et al. 2019, 1) by erasing Black and Indigenous voices from the Plantationocene discourse (Jegathesan 2021, 80).

The above ethnographic findings from Assam suggests that the Plantationocene's point of inflection and marking of a new era obscure important continuities. In Assam, the intersection of structural casteism (including its oppressive dyadic structuring principles of purity and impurity) and economic precarity are carried in the bodies of Adivasis and Dalits when they move to and from plantations.[7] The ethnographic evidence provided above demonstrates how casteism constitutes a major structuring principle beyond plantations—for instance, in rural India where Raju wants to move because caste hierarchies are still in place and Adivasis and Dalits are spatially separated from caste Hindus, unlike those living on plantations in Assam. Structural discriminations based on ethnicity and caste are also prevalent in tea workers' trade unionism, when Adivasis and Dalits are excluded from leadership positions in trade unions as much as in state policies, excluding historically discriminated Adivasis from affirmative action in Assam. Thus, understanding the plantations as permeable spaces rather than enclaves draws attention to the continuities of forms of injustice beyond the

Plantationocene and calls for a different scale by which to address justice affecting plantation economies.[8]

Justice Beyond Plantation "Enclaves"

This chapter has described the basic characteristics of the indentured labor system under which migrant laborers were recruited in the nineteenth and early twentieth centuries, and it discussed labor mobility to and from Assam tea plantations under the labor law regime of the Plantations Labour Act after Indian independence. I have illustrated that labor migration did not stop with Indian independence, as suggested in long-bygone migration narratives, but continued well into the second half of the twentieth century. Laborers in postcolonial India are not legally forced by British colonialists to migrate to plantations or to stay on plantations. Rather, they are driven by precarious livelihoods off the plantations to migrate to Assam and seek wage labor on plantations. At the same time, tea laborers and their children embrace various forms of mobility away from the tea plantations, including subsistence farming, temporary work in India's metropolitan cities, and activist engagements. Since farming is often not sufficient to make ends meet, former laborers who leave plantation work to engage in farming are often forced to seek additional wage employment, and many end up back on plantations, as temporary laborers and under worse labor conditions than before. Therefore, spatial mobility sometimes turns into downward social mobility. Temporary labor migration to India's metropolitan cities is evaluated differently but ultimately does not lead to sustainable upward social mobility for those who eventually become plantation laborers again after returning from the cities. The main opportunity to gain upward socioeconomic mobility for tea laborers' offspring is through labor rights activism, which is, however, only available to a few.

Based on the ethnographic evidence I have gathered of ongoing mobility to and from Assam tea plantations, I suggest conceptualizing plantations as fluid, permeable, and transforming spaces rather than enclosed, unchanged enclaves. Like Tiffany Lethabo King (2019) and Mythri Jegathesan (2019), who suggest new imagined geographies through the metaphor of the "pore" and the "*poēsis* of desire," respectively, which constitute "productive frictions" (Lethabo King 2019, 19), I attempt an epistemic move to create new foci in studies of plantation work. Moving beyond equating plantations with "enclaves" recalibrates taken-for-granted foci on plantations that obscure spatial mobility. This shift beyond the enclave frame echoes the call of Andreas Wimmer and Nina Glick Schiller (2002, 302) to move beyond "methodological nationalism"—"the assumption that the nation/state/society is the natural social and political form of the modern world." Similarly, equalizing plantations with "enclaves" has naturalized an analytical view on plantation labor as immobile, bounded, and fixed. "Methodological enclavism" has obscured the fact that plantations are transforming and permeable spaces that provide a refuge for workers and their dependents who frequently move to and from plantations without gaining substantial upward social mobility.

Regarding justice imaginaries, "methodological enclavism" rests on the premise that the scale on which to discuss labor justice is the plantation enclave. When defining plantations as the scale to address matters of labor justice, either British or Indian planters are defined as the agents who are responsible for implementing labor justice to tea laborers, or it is considered that problems of injustice resolve when the plantation economies cease to exist. While the methodological enclavism perspective on justice allows for the identification of clearly identifiable responsible agents of justice (tea planters), it does not consider how caste and class oppression determine tea laborers' experiences when they are heading for subsistence farming, temporary jobs in metropolitan cities, or trade unionism and activism. Even if tea plantations eventually cease to exist, it is doubtful that the world without "old-style" plantations will be a better world for tea laborers in Assam and beyond since the injustice and inequality of economic exploitation and structural casteism still exist, even more so, beyond the plantation. When upscaling questions of justice beyond the plantation enclave to consider economic exploitation and structural casteism beyond Assam tea plantations, it becomes obvious that replacing "old-style" tea plantations with another political economy of tea production is not necessarily bringing more justice to tea laborers. Therefore, justice works differently when addressed at different scales that highlight certain aspects of justice while disregarding others.

LIVING FROM THE TEA LEAVES

Tea plantation life in Assam has often been presented in "killer stories" (Jegath-esan 2019, 35), in which labor rights violations, such as the lack of sanitary, housing, medical, educational, and protective facilities, are highlighted (e.g., Banerji and Willoughby 2019; Columbia Law School Human Rights Institute 2014; Ray 2016; Rowlatt and Deith 2015; Xaxa 1996). While killer stories serve as a useful political tool to fight against human rights violations, they somehow overshadow the complexities of people's everyday lives on Assam tea plantations by reading tea plantation life through the narrow lens of rights violation.

"Everyday life" (de Certeau 2013; Lefebvre 2014) or "ordinariness" is a common theme that has drawn its way through different intellectual traditions. The everyday is the adjective characterizing various research topics such as "everyday resistance" (Scott 1985, 1990) or "everyday justice" (Brunnegger 2019). The everyday is a "situated sense-making essence of social order" (Marcus 1993, 244) or the "context for the text we provide" (Dumm 1999, 1). In colloquial language, "ordinary" or "everyday" have often been understood as the opposite of the eventful, something that is taken for granted, commonsensical, recurring, and predictable (Dumm 1999, 1). In theories of the everyday, on the other hand, influenced by ordinary language philosophy (e.g., Cavell 1986), the uncanniness or the indeterminacy of the ordinary has been emphasized more recently by Veena Das (2007, 2018a, 2018b, 2020) and others (e.g., Kelly 2008; Khan 2010). The everyday is characterized as heterogeneous, dynamic, elusive, complex, unpredictable, and contingent (Brunnegger 2019, 5–8). It is seen as the (sometimes surprising) result of a process of normalization rather than being a given. For some, the maintenance of everyday life constitutes hard labor.[1]

This chapter describes an ordinary working day on a tea plantation in Assam from the perspective of Jiya—a tea plucker on Dolani Tea Estate. It illustrates how Jiya navigates her everyday life structured by the company's relentless siren and her relationship to the plantation. Everyday life on tea plantations is characterized by habitual repetition as well as laborers' loyalty toward the tea companies because laborers "live from the tea leaves." However, tea plantation laborers also use their capacity to act differently (Giddens 1984, 9) to break through structural patterns of givenness. This chapter is closely related to the next chapter on why tea laborers do (not) rebel. Over the course of the two chapters, I develop the argument that justice works in context. While loyalty toward tea companies and the old-style plantation economy works structure-maintaining under the old political economy of Assam tea (described in the introduction), it demonstrates structure-undermining workings of justice when placed in the currently transforming political economy of Assam tea. The photos, the plantation, the protagonist, and the incidents described in this chapter are based on real places, persons, and observations, but their compilation from multiple observations into one day is a work of fiction.

First Siren: Time to Get Up

Jiya woke up late, at five o'clock in the morning, one day in November, when the company's relentless siren awoke the plantation with its howling, jarring sound. Jiya started her daily routine by washing yesterday's dishes, since the water supply had already stopped by the time her family had finished dinner the previous night. Before daybreak, still wearing her loose nightgown, she stepped out into the dark street in front of her house, while her husband and children were still asleep. Holding the dirty dishes in her hands, she walked toward one of the two watering places on her street. Unfortunately, two women had been faster than Jiya, so she had to wait. "I just got up too late today," she said ruefully. When it was her turn, she tied up her ankle-length nightgown to prevent it from getting wet and started to wash the dishes using a wadded wisp of straw as a dish sponge and solidified ashes from the kitchen stove as detergent. After cleaning the dishes, Jiya quickly washed herself at the same water spot.

Jiya was about thirty-two years old at that time. She lived with her husband and two children, aged twelve and sixteen, in a labor line on Dolani Tea Estate. The workers called her labor line the "Baptist church line" since the church was on that road. The labor line was close to the central marketplace, where a few shops were located and where the weekly markets and important events took place. Labor lines are usually spread out all over a tea plantation. In Dolani Tea Estate, however, all the labor lines were positioned together around the central marketplace. Jiya grew up on Dolani Tea Estate as the daughter of a tea plucker and a factory worker. Jiya's father had died long ago. Her mother had retired a couple of years earlier and had fallen seriously ill since. The mother lived with one of Jiya's brothers in the upper labor lines. Jiya had married when she was only fifteen years old and had worked on the plantation for almost two decades. "I understood early what it means to suffer," she once commented.

After Jiya had hurried back to her house from the water pit that day, she lit a fire in her kitchen—a room attached to her three-room house with a mud floor, bamboo walls, and a corrugated iron roof (fig. 1). The kitchen was almost empty, except for the firepit, which Jiya had built barehanded from bricks and clad with a mixture of clay and cow dung. She had left two vents in her construction—one in front and one on top—so that she could make a fire in the front opening. She gradually added the firewood, partly provided by her company and partly collected from the woods. The opening on top was used to place a pot over the fire. Jiya washed some rice and put it on her self-made fire stove.

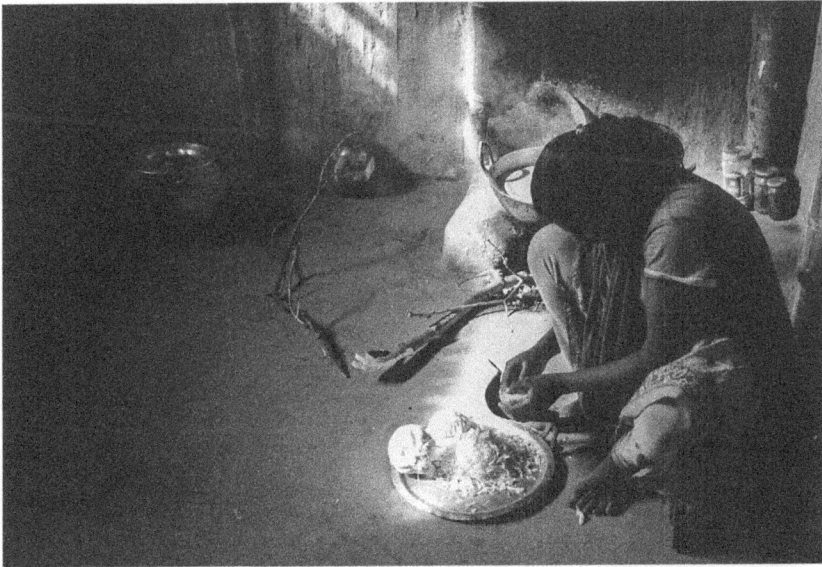

FIGURE 1.   A tea plantation laborer's kitchen. Photo by the author, Assam 2015.

Second Siren: Getting Ready for Work

When Jiya slipped into her house after putting the rice on the stove, the second company siren rang out at six o'clock, exhorting her and all the other laborers to get ready for work. Jiya woke her two children to get them ready for school and dressed herself in an old sari. Her daughter was in class eight in a governmental Assamese-medium school in a nearby town. Her son was in class five in a private English-medium school. He aspired to become a YouTube star once he grew up like other young people from the plantation (fig. 2).

FIGURE 2. A tea plantation laborer's son presenting his YouTube channel. Photo by the author, Assam 2023.

Neither Jiya nor her husband had ever attended school. Jiya regretted that her parents had never let her go to school. Like many other women, she had been obliged to help her mother with the housework and take care of her brothers, and she had started working when she was just thirteen years old to support the family with some extra income. Jiya's only sister had died as a child. Her two brothers were allowed to attend school; however, one was not interested in it, and the other had dropped out at some point. Jiya's husband worked as an electrician for the tea company and had fluctuating working hours since he worked in shifts. Sometimes he did not feel like working at all. He aspired to work as an electrician outside the plantation, convinced he could earn much more for the same kind of work.

Jiya combed her hair in front of a small mirror with a yellow plastic frame (fig. 3). She also applied some purple lipstick. "To prevent the dry cold cracking my lips," she said to herself. Suddenly, she knelt in the middle of the room, pulled the long edge of her dark green sari over her head, and uttered a prayer. When she got up, she commented, "I should not forget to be thankful since my life was gifted to me and for what I have." Jiya was born into a Hindu family but had converted to Christianity after she married her husband, whose family was Baptist.

Jiya's rice in the kitchen was now ready to eat. She kept the rice water aside to drink later and served her children rice for breakfast with some leftover vegetables

FIGURE 3. Tea laborer dressing in front of a mirror. Photo by the author, Assam 2016.

from the night before. Vegetables meant potatoes. For lunch, she packed the same food for her children and herself. Instead of eating, Jiya had just tea for breakfast, which the company provided for her. On top of that, she washed down some Ayurvedic medicine with hot rice water to stave off the sensation of hunger. In the absence of milk and sugar, Jiya drank her tea black with salt, noting that "it would taste better with sugar" while stroking her spindly thin belly.

Third Siren: Brisk Steps to Work

Just as Jiya was collecting her working utensils in her big bamboo basket and strapping it onto her back, the siren rang for the third time, indicating that it was seven o'clock—the official start of work. Jiya stepped out of her house hastily, dawn having already broken its hazy light into the day. She went past the market-place toward the garden section of the plantation. In the left corner of the mar-ketplace, a barber sat in front of his hair salon on a bench, reading the newspaper. The barber looked up and gave a friendly greeting. Next to his salon was a small restaurant selling samosas, triangular fried dumplings with savory fillings, and jalebis, deep-fried flour batter in spirals. As usual, there were no indoor guests in the restaurant since workers bought samosas and jalebis only to take away for special occasions. On the right side of the marketplace were several small stores selling basic food and hygiene products. Every store had a low wooden shop counter facing the marketplace, decorated with lined-up plastic boxes of candy for one rupee each.

Jiya took a left turn after the marketplace. A vivid hustle and bustle of hun-dreds of laborers hurrying to work in different directions filled the roads. The younger ones rode on bicycles, ringing their bells playfully while overtaking the older ones walking. Before the big crossroad in front of the factory, Jiya suddenly turned into a small lane (fig. 4) to prevent bumping into the overseer, because he would have scolded her for being late. Jiya laughed into her sleeve for escaping the overseer successfully.

In front of Jiya, a water sprinkler irrigated the fields. Some water reached her track, so she ran to avoid the water jets. When one water jet hit her nonetheless, Jiya burst into laughter, and the women walking past her joined in. After about two to three kilometers of brisk steps, Jiya reached the garden section where her group was plucking tea. Laborers usually chose themselves which working group they wanted to join when they started their work on the plantation. Most laborers chose working groups with relatives, neighbors, or friends wherefore the com-position of work groups resembled social relations beyond the working group.

FIGURE 4. Tea pluckers carrying collected firewood in a labor line. Photo by the author, Assam 2015.

In the Fields

When Jiya arrived at the garden, most of the women in her unit had already started working. One could see people's heads poking out of the wide green fields of tea bushes in different positions in their lanes. Jiya quickly put on an old, ragged, outsized shirt on top of her sari to protect it from getting worn out. Additionally, she wrapped a striped rag around her hips, which she tied with a rope, covering her from toe to belly to protect her clothes and body against dirt, humid leaves, and harm from tea branches or biting insects. Jiya placed another small rag on her head—against the cold in the morning, against the sun as the day progressed, and to make the weight of her basket feel less heavy. Finally, she placed the strap of her tea basket on top of her head, so she could carry the basket for collecting the tea leaves on her back. She entered one lane, approached her small group, and started plucking leaves. The tea bushes reached up to Jiya's hips. Each tea bush had one thick trunk from which several small branches spread out. Since tea bushes were planted close to one another and pruned evenly in the shape of a "plucking table," they looked more like one even surface than separate plants. The lower tea leaves were resilient and had a dark green color. Tea pluckers were trained to pluck only the soft, light green tea leaves that grew freshly on the tea bushes' "plucking table"—those famous two leaves and a bud. Jiya plucked the tea leaves with both hands by turning the palms of her hands down, snatching the fresh leaves between her fingers, and tearing them out in one go (fig. 5). She tore as many leaves as her hands could hold and then threw a handful of leaves over her shoulder into the basket on her back. She plucked so quickly that her hands seemed to float up and down over the bushes.

There were few leaves that day, because November constitutes the end of the annual plucking period. The overseer urged the pluckers to only pick the small leaves, although they were scarce. At the same time, the company put pluckers under pressure to pluck at least twenty-four kilos of green leaves per day to receive their full wage. If laborers did not manage to pluck the required kilos, half of their wages could be deducted. When they could pluck more than the daily target, they got paid extra money per kilo. In the high seasons for tea, good pluckers sometimes managed to pluck one hundred kilos of tea leaves per day, while others struggled to reach the minimum target at less fertile times of the year. Jiya was one of the efficient pluckers who earned extra income in the high seasons by plucking extra leaves. She once showed me her and her husband's pay slips proudly to demonstrate that she earned more than him.

On that day, however, Anita, a plucker in Jiya's small group, accused Jiya of plucking the bigger leaves in addition to the small ones to reach her daily target more easily. Anita told Jiya, "Look at my leaves, they are small and beautiful like

FIGURE 5. Woman plucking tea. Photo by the author, Assam 2016.

rice!" Jiya protested that she would never cheat and had been falsely accused by Anita. Jiya insisted she always tried her best and was completely trustworthy: "We workers live from the tea leaves. I know that the company's management must sell the leaves. So, if the leaves are good, it is also good for us. If we do not work properly, it is also not good for us." When Jiya collected her daily target of twenty-four kilos of fresh leaves, her tea company could create six to eight kilos of ready-processed tea leaves for sale. Jiya earned Rs. 137—about $1.90—per day in cash in 2015. Her company would sell one kilo of her processed tea by auction for about Rs. 140.

At around nine o'clock, the first tea leaf weighing took place. A mohara, a lower-level supervisor, dropped by on his motorcycle. He arranged a suspended scale between three wooden bamboo stakes in the middle of the road (fig. 6). Behind the scale, pluckers formed a line to wait for their turn. Jiya queued with the other pluckers after transferring her tea leaves from her basket into a nylon bag, which had more space and was easier to weigh. The mohara stood next to the scale and wrote down how many kilos of leaves each plucker had collected on his yellow notepad. He knew every woman by name and by the number that the company had assigned for administrative purposes.

It was easy to spot the mohara among the laborers. He was wearing casual pants, a shirt, and sneakers, together with an expensive-looking branded wrist-

FIGURE 6. Suspended scale for weighing tea leaves. Photo by the author, Assam 2016.

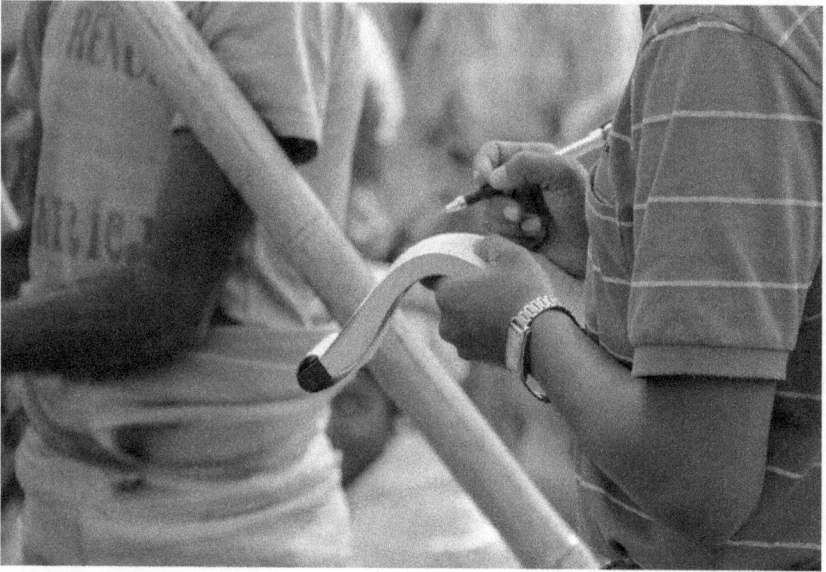

FIGURE 7. A mohara taking notes of the amount of collected tea leaves. Photo by the author, Assam 2016.

watch—symbols that indicated his better economic status and distinguished him from the "ordinary" laborers (fig. 7). Moreover, his physical appearance indicated that he did not have to suffer hunger in his life. Moharas were often the children of tea plantation laborers who had benefited from above-average education. Some came from outside the plantations and obtained their jobs through official application procedures. Moharas earned about five times as much as tea laborers and were given better facilities, including superior houses, cleaner drinking water, full-time electricity, gas stoves, and so forth.

When it was Jiya's turn, she hoisted her heavy bag full of leaves with both hands to hang it on the suspended scale. The scale showed that she had collected seven kilos this morning, but she did not pay attention to the measurement because she was busy quickly taking her bag down and moving on to make way for the next plucker waiting for her turn. The mohara stimulated a high pace by calling the next woman's name and number even before Jiya had fully grabbed her bag from the suspended scale. She placed the bag on her head and moved on to a red midget tractor waiting at some distance. Three male field laborers collated all the leaves in front of the tractor. They emptied Jiya's nylon bag into an even bigger nylon bag of the same kind. To stuff as many leaves as possible into one big bag, one of the field workers pressed the leaves deep into the bag with his bare feet. When a bag was full, the field workers placed it onto the tractor's trailer.

FIGURE 8.   Tea pluckers accessing a water tank. Photo by the author, Assam 2016.

After dumping her tea leaves, Jiya moved on to the water tanks, which provided cold fresh water and hot, salted tea. Jiya pushed herself in front of the water tap with her coworkers and reached for the water jet to clean her feet, hands, and face. Then, she took an old plastic bottle and filled it with drinking water for herself. All the workers shared the same water tap (fig. 8), which in some parts of India would be unthinkable due to caste hierarchies.

When Jiya moved back slowly to the garden to continue plucking, the tractor driver started his engine and drove off to deliver the leaves to the company's factory for further processing. Jiya's collected fresh tea leaves would be processed into orthodox or crush, tear, curl (CTC) black tea. Factory workers received the leaves from the field workers and spread them out on a fine grid for six to twelve hours to wilt. Hot air was pumped in through huge ventilators until the leaves' moisture had reduced by 70 percent. For CTC processing, which accounts for 90 percent of the tea produced in India (Rajya Sabha 2012, 3), tea leaves were rolled, pressed, and torn, to break the cell walls; the juice was wrung from the leaves; and a chemical reaction to oxidation was started, in which essential oils oxidized from the leaf to the air. Afterward, the leaves were laid out to rest for several hours in cool, moist air. Here, the main oxidation took place, which turned the tea leaves from dark green into a reddish-brown color and changed their chemical composition, because the oxygen in the air interacted with the now-exposed enzymes in the leaf. A quick drying and heating of the leaves with hot air stopped the chemical reaction that had been unleashed by the preceding oxidation process and reduced the leaves' moisture to lower than 3 percent. At the end, the tea leaves were sorted by size through screening. Ready-processed CTC tea took the shape of small-hackled crumbs, which are typically used to prepare Indian chai, since CTC tea has a strong flavor. Orthodox tea, on the other hand, is produced by maintaining the wholeness and integrity of the tea leaf. Its taste and color are light—similar to traditional Chinese tea. Most orthodox teas in India are produced in Darjeeling. The orthodox teas produced in Assam were almost exclusively exported, and their sale prices were much higher than those for CTC tea. Three to four kilos of fresh tea leaves were manufactured into one kilo of processed tea. Fresh tea leaves were collected and weighed three times a day—at nine, twelve, and four o'clock. After the second weighing, pluckers had about an hour's lunch break.

Fourth Siren: Lunch Break

Jiya sat with Anita and the other pluckers from her small group for lunch. They formed a circle in the middle of a dusty road that separated two garden sections. Jiya untied the rope around her hips and loosened the fabric she had wrapped around her body while plucking. She spread the fabric on the ground to sit on. She opened her bag, in which she kept her lunchbox—quite a big stainless-steel bucket full of rice, together with a small number of potatoes on top. Her lunchbox looked like those of the other group members—in shape and content (fig. 9).

Jiya placed the lid of her box carefully in front of her, got up, and walked around with her bucket to share a tiny amount of her potatoes. The other women in her group did the same. After everybody had shared parts of their lunch, each woman had a mixture of differently prepared vegetables on her bucket's lid, although the variety was limited to potatoes and spinach.

After lunch, everybody relaxed a bit. Some women in Jiya's group combed and dressed someone else's hair. The conversations revolved around daily issues: "My daughter-in-law prepared food this morning." "There was no water at four o'clock this morning, so I went to sleep again for an hour." "I have pains everywhere." "The tea bushes do not provide good leaves today." "Why didn't Rita come to work today?" "My daughter needs to get married soon." "I have not seen the manager (baṛā sāhib) for a few days." And so on.

Everybody listened carefully when one woman shared that she had heard about a woman and her unborn baby who had died the night before. She told the others that the pregnant woman had gone to the hospital because her baby

FIGURE 9.   Nylon bags containing tea pluckers' lunchboxes. Photo by the author, Assam 2016.

was about to be born. Only one doctor was employed on the plantation, and he spent very little time in the hospital, apart from two consultation hours each afternoon. The rest of the time, one or another nurse or helper was responsible for overseeing the hospital. Moreover, medical equipment and medications were limited. The woman narrated that the pregnant woman had faced difficulties in her labor the previous night. When the nurse present could not reach the doctor, they had transported her to the next tea plantation's hospital, where a doctor was available, in the company's ambulance. However, the pregnant woman and her baby did not survive the journey.

After the lunch break, Jiya and the other women reluctantly returned to work. Although the winter season was about to start, and the morning hours were already getting cold, the sun was boiling after lunch. Jiya struck up one song after another as a pastime to overcome her boredom—popular Bollywood songs and *bhajan* devotional songs. Jiya also hid between tea bushes to take a small break by disappearing from the overseers' sight. The last weighing took place at four o'clock. The pluckers had to wait for this last weighing because they wanted to add the tea leaves they had collected from their afternoon working hours. On some plantations, laborers complained that the company conducted the last weighing even later than four o'clock to force laborers to work overtime—especially during the high seasons. On that day, however, the final weighing was on time.

Fifth Siren: End of the Workday

Afterward, Jiya and the others swarmed back home. Walking home could take half an hour to an hour, depending on the work section's distance to the labor lines, which changed daily. As Jiya walked home, she said to her neighbor, "You don't feel like walking so far after a day of work, do you?" Her neighbor nodded in agreement.

As Jiya reached the marketplace, she saw lots of people standing in front of the labor club, a small building that the company provided to the laborers for meetings, to watch TV, or just to hang out. The people were talking across one another excitedly. Jiya approached the crowd and tried to figure out what was going on. The local president from the All Adivasi Students' Association, one of the main interest groups working on behalf of tea plantation laborers in Assam, told her that a girl from a neighboring plantation had been "kidnapped by an agent" who wanted to take her to Delhi for work. "Another case of human trafficking," the president concluded, slipping back into the labor club. Jiya decided to go home since she needed to get some housework done. As she walked to her house, she became very angry, as her daughter had recently been kidnapped, along with another girl. Almost every family on the Dolani Tea Estate had a family member who had been kidnapped in that way.

Jiya's daughter had decided herself to leave the plantation with an agent without informing her parents. Jiya supposed that her daughter must have been bewitched by one of the witches on the plantation, since she could not imagine how her daughter would have been capable of running away otherwise. The other girl was the daughter of Jiya's husband's elder brother. When the girls disappeared, Jiya's husband borrowed a mohara's motorbike to search for the girls. After a few days of driving around, he found them on a neighboring plantation. They had planned to hide for a few days on the plantation before moving on to reduce the chances of being caught on the way. Jiya's husband brought the girls back safely, but when he was on his way to bring the motorcycle back to the mohara, he had an accident. Nothing happened to him, but the motorcycle got severely damaged. Jiya estimated that the whole searching efforts had cost her family around Rs. 15,000—which was equal to almost five months of Jiya's cash payment. They took some money from the annual bonus that tea companies pay to laborers once a year during the festival season in October. Jiya and her husband's bonus amounted to about Rs. 5,000 each.

The remaining Rs. 5,000, they took from their hundi group. Jiya and her husband "played" hundi because they did not have a bank account for savings.[2] They got together with a group of laborers for a fixed period for a hundi. The size of the groups varies as well as the duration of each hundi. One hundi takes the same number of weeks as people participate. Everyone in the hundi group pays a weekly amount of money—usually around two hundred rupees—to the person in charge. Everybody is then eligible to receive the full amount of money from all participants once during a hundi. The group decides each week anew who should get the money according to individual needs. One woman once commented, "In that way the money gets saved for when you need it. Saving the money in the house never works. There is always one or the other thing that you need. Imagine the oil gets empty and you do not have any money left except for the money that you wanted to keep. You would just take the money and buy oil then. But if no money is left in the house, you just survive without oil till you get paid again."

Jiya and her husband took the hundi money to cover the costs of the searching efforts for their daughter and their niece although the hundi money was already scheduled to pay their son's annual school fees. Jiya requested her husband's brother to pay them half of the money, which they had spent to bring the two girls back, since it was also his daughter they saved. Yet, the father of the girl refused to give them any money. Jiya wanted to talk to the trade union president and ask him for his help. If this would not help, Jiya wanted to move to the company's welfare manager for help. The incident of another girl who was taken to be brought to Delhi for work on that day made Jiya emotional because she remembered her own fateful experience with her daughter. After Jiya's husband found and returned their daughter, they had sent her to his relatives who live some one hundred kilometers away. They made her stay with the relatives until the worst gossiping had calmed down.

Housework

When Jiya reached her house after work, it was already past five. Since it gets dark early in the latitudinal lines where the plantations in Assam are located, Jiya worried about finishing her housework quickly. Reaching her house, she dropped her working utensils and washed her feet and hands properly. "The garden is so dirty," she said. Washing her feet after plucking also helped to relieve the unpleasant itching that is an ordinary concomitant of working between tea bushes. Jiya hurried back and forth around the house to get the housework done as quickly as possible. She took the dishes she had used for breakfast to the watering place and cleaned everything. When she returned, she cleaned the house floor with a handmade broom. In the meantime, Jiya's husband and son played carom in the garden.

Before Jiya started her preparations for dinner, she took a bath. There was a vivid hustle and bustle around the watering place since so many women needed water simultaneously after work. Jiya wrapped a thin cotton towel around her wet hair after bathing. Her whole body shivered from the cold. The water provided came from the nearby mountains and was extremely cold. Jiya rubbed her shaking hands in front of her body and blew some air from her mouth into her hands to feel warmer. She carried buckets of water to her kitchen and started cooking with her daughter's help. Her son had collected the weekly food ration from the company's distribution center that day.[3] Jiya was excited to make roti tonight since the company's whole wheat flour ration was never sufficient for a whole week and had previously run out. While she prepared bread and vegetables for dinner, neighbors visited. Jiya's husband and son were watching TV and entertaining the guests. Jiya had to stop cooking to prepare tea for the visitors since the fire stove had only one hob. During the winter days, it was pleasant to spend time in front of the fire to stay warm, and sometimes the whole family gathered around the firepit in the kitchen during the evening while the food was being prepared, although the thick smoke made their eyes burn after a while.

Jiya's family gathered in front of the TV for dinner that evening. The pleasant smell of flame-grilled hot bread filled the house while they ate. They watched a news channel. A few weeks previously, Indian Prime Minister Narendra Modi had announced the demonetization of five hundred– and one thousand–rupee notes, and the news was reporting on people waiting in long lines in front of ATMs to take out their money. While they were watching TV, the electricity cut out several times. As Jiya lit a candle and placed it on the table, the candlelight broke the complete darkness. After dinner, Jiya and her family members got ready to sleep. It was only seven thirty in the evening, but her day would start early again tomorrow. She would try to get up before five o'clock—early enough to avoid queuing at the water spot again.

Maintaining Everyday Life

The fictional ordinary working day on Dolani Tea Estate through the eyes of the tea plucker Jiya introduces tea laborers' position vis-à-vis other differently positioned actors on Assam tea plantations. It shows the circumstances of deprivation and hardship that tea laborers must deal with daily—making every day on a tea plantation not simply a given but hard maintaining work. The narrative also hints at tea plantation laborers' odds to act differently (Giddens 1984, 9) to break through structural patterns of givenness—for instance, when Jiya turned into a small lane to prevent bumping into the overseer when she was running late, or her hiding between tea bushes to take a small unnoticed break from work. The narrative illustrates the multifaceted gendered nature of plantation work and life that others have dealt with in more detail (e.g., Chatterjee 2001; Chaudhuri 2013; Besky 2014; Banerjee 2014). In global comparison, India has one of the lowest women labor force participation rates. According to the International Labor Organization, the global average women labor force participation rate for women older than fifteen years amounted to 48.7 percent in 2023. The Indian women labor force participation rate, on the contrary, amounted to only 32.7 percent for the same year.[4] Against the background of these statistics, the fact that almost half of the tea plantation laborers in Assam were female (Mishra et al. 2012, 96) is remarkable and has complex and ambiguous implications for gender relations on the plantations.[5] On the one hand, women on plantations have more freedom to move around by themselves and with friends compared to many women living in India outside the plantation context. Women on plantations also earn at least as much as their husbands, often even more because of the additional benefits they receive during the high seasons for plucking above the prescribed minimum amount of leaves. This makes women workers relatively independent from male breadwinners financially. On the other hand, as Jiya's example illustrates, women often did most of the housework and care work on top of their labor for the tea companies, which created a heavy work overload for many women. While Jiya was busy cleaning the house and preparing dinner, her husband and son played carom in the garden. Women like Jiya often cut down their food consumption to save money for the children's education, which frequently results in severe health issues related to malnutrition. Women are more likely to be convinced not to go to school or to drop out of school in order to help their mothers with the care work and housework, and as soon as they are old enough also work to financially support the family with extra income. The structural position of women tea laborers is different from a (heterogenous) majority of housewives in India and from an (equally heterogenous) emerging women working middle class in urban centers (Brosius 2016). It challenges, as others (e.g., Banerjee 2021, Sen 2017) have argued, dichotomies between freedom and unfreedom.

The women tea workers' loyalty to the tea companies illustrated in this chapter must be understood against their outlined structural position on Assam tea plantations. Jiya's insistence that she would never cheat because she lived from the tea leaves is an expression of deep loyalty toward tea companies and tea plantations. In the next chapter, which is closely related to the present chapter, I develop the argument that loyalty toward tea companies as part of holding onto the old-style plantation economy works structure-maintaining under the old political economy of Assam tea but demonstrates structure-undermining workings of justice when placed in the currently transforming political economy of Assam tea.

WHY TEA PLANTATION LABORERS DO (NOT) REBEL

I was up by five o'clock one morning in December 2015 to join two of my tea laborer acquaintances for pruning work. There are four annual seasons (or "flushes") for Assam tea between March and November, while the three months from December to February constitute the offseason when tea bushes are pruned. Pruning is hard manual work. I met Asha and Rajni at a crossing close to the factory, and Rajni took me on the back of her bicycle to the area allocated for pruning for that day.

As we reached the lower garden section where we were supposed to prune, the sardar of Asha and Rajni's group instructed each worker where to start working. Rajni was told to prune the first two bush arrays bordering the road, while Asha and other workers were instructed to prune the bushes deeper inside the gardens. Rajni was given a special task because the overseer thought that she pruned better than the others. Thus, if the manager came along to check the quality of the pruning work, he would get a better impression of the work on the face of it and be less likely to complain too harshly. Rajni walked toward the first bush in her array. She closed her eyes, lifted her pruning knife, which she held tight between her hands, in front of her face, and mumbled a prayer. Rajni was from a Gwala caste Hindu family of comparatively high status on the plantation. Her best friend Asha was from a lower caste, and Rajni sometimes made jokes that if they lived in other parts of India, she would never enter Asha's house or eat at the same table with her. In Dolani Tea Estate, they became close friends across caste hierarchies. Maybe they felt connected because of their difficult family fates.

Asha was married, but her husband had died from an alcohol overdose and left her as a childless widow in her early twenties. Rajni's father had died early and since her elder brother refused to work and her mother was sick, Rajni became the family's breadwinner even before she turned twenty. It took Rajni about two minutes to prune the first bush. During the early morning hours, pruning was comparatively easy because the bushes' branches are still covered in moisture from the morning dew and are therefore softer.

Rajni complained that the manager came every single day to check their work and usually found something or other to nag about. She said that the previous manager had never done this. "The former manager was all right compared to the present one," Rajni concluded. Two sardars, one mohara, and the jamadar babu were present that day to supervise the work. The sardars instructed the women to improve their pruning and helped them when they fell behind. The mohara and the jamadar babu ran through the arrays shouting, "Work hard!" and "Do good work!" or "Cut the bushes exactly to one level!" Suddenly a man drove by on his motorbike. The women whispered "Sahab . . . sahab came . . ." to one another. I later got to know that this "sahab" (i.e., Sir) was the newly appointed assistant manager who had started to work on Dolani Tea Estate just a few days earlier. The sahab got down from his bike and inspected a few bushes in the front arrays. The jamadar babu talked to him nervously at the roadside before he got on his bike again and drove away.

The workers had finished pruning around a hundred big bushes in the meantime, which was one third of their daily task. The highest-ranking overseer turned toward the workers and shouted, "You did not do a good job today! You did not prune the bushes to the same level! You have to come back and prune all the bushes again!" A loud murmur went through the crowd and the workers started to talk across one another. Rajni, Asha, and a few other workers walked out of the field toward the road. Slowly but surely, all workers followed them one after the other. There were about a hundred workers altogether. They sat down on the road. The overseers ran across the street furiously, screaming, "Get up immediately! Quickly, start working again!" None of the workers moved an inch. The overseers became rough, slapping the workers lightly on their shoulders or the backs of their heads while constantly repeating, "Get up! Work!" The workers, unimpressed by the overseers' vigorousness, remained seated and shrieked back, "We will not go back to work!" This confrontation went on for quite some time before the workers finally went back to work.

Injustice, James Scott (1976, 158) argued, can only be perceived if people have a norm of justice in mind from which it has departed. Based on this premise, this chapter analyzes instances during my fieldwork in which tea plantation laborers decided to protest—in more or less visible ways—because they felt treated unjustly. Following Scott, I examine these instances in order to understand underlying norms of justice. I argue that laborers claimed appropriate remuneration for their efforts in mainly nonmonetary terms, such as acknowledgment, and often did not aim toward radical transformations; instead, they aimed toward maintaining proper relations within the "old-style" tea plantation welfare economy. Therefore, while their protests "are intended to mitigate or deny claims made by superordinate classes" (Scott 1985, 32), the hegemonic order itself is not being challenged as such but is being used to criticize elites that do not act according to the rules of their hegemonic order (Scott 1990). The aim of maintaining instead of subverting the hegemonic order can further be seen in the fact that laborers' protests constituted the exception rather than a rule. Protest studies' popular question of "why [wo]men rebel" (Gurr 1970) is therefore turned upside down.

The chapter is divided into three sections. First, I introduce the history of labor protest based on historical accounts of Assam tea plantations. Second, I analyze three instances of (everyday) protest among tea plantation workers in order to illustrate my argument that laborers' underlying justice regimes are informed by the old-style plantation economy. Instead of dismissing laborers' desire to maintain proper work relations in the old-style political economy of tea production as reactionary, I state in the third section that adhering to this labor law regime during its gradual replacement by a new labor law regime transforms working modes of justice. When norms of justice are placed in a different context—here, a changing political economy of tea production—their function also changes. Under the old plantation economy, the justice regime shaped by the Plantations Labour Act operated in a system-preserving and rectifying manner. However, in the emerging political economy, the same justice regime functions in a structure-undermining way. In other words, while the fundamental objects of justice remain unchanged, their operation is context-dependent.

Earlier studies on labor resistance on tea plantations (e.g., Banerjee 2017) and beyond (Scott 1990) have shown that resistance is often not against hegemonic structures but operates within it. Building on these theories from the perspective of *justice at work*, I argue that both critique and maintenance of structures can be understood as forms of agency. Laborers did not "misrecognize" their *actually* exploitative labor relations on the plantation as beneficial due to "false consciousness" (76), nor were they *actually* expressing a desire for a better future for their children by romanticizing the bygone *industri* model of plantations (Besky 2014). Rather, many laborers, like Rajni and Asha, recognized that maintaining the old-style plantation economy was the better option at a time of radical transformations in the political economy of tea production, when their labor was on the line.

Histories of Tea Labor Resistance

Tea plantation laborers' protest in pre-independence Assam has gained attention in a few historical studies (see, e.g., Behal 2014 and Varma 2011). The Indian historian Rana Behal distinguishes different phases of labor protest on plantations in Assam while taking changing historical settings into account. In the absence of laborers' own recorded testimonies, Behal mainly relied on planters' written accounts as well as documents of colonial administrative correspondence.

During what Behal categorizes as the first phase of resistance in the mid-nineteenth century, the tea industry was not yet financially stable and there were not enough laborers available, especially to increase the acreage for tea planting and open new tea estates. Companies delayed payments to laborers and tried to reduce their wages and increase their workload to maximize the profits needed to establish the industry. The first strike, according to Behal, was reported in 1848 when tea laborers stopped working and gathered outside a company's office to protest delayed wage payments and increased workload. In what followed, laborers continued to protest tea planters' exploitative profit-maximizing strategies— for example, by deserting before their contracts had ended. This was possible because laborers had more attractive alternatives at that time, such as infrastructural work, which was better paid (Behal 2014, 268–289).

Behal (2014) dates the second phase of labor resistance to the 1860s, after the enforcement of the Workmen's Breach of Contract Act in 1859 and Act VI of the Bengal Council of 1865, which introduced the indentured labor system (see chap. 2). During the 1860s, Assam tea planters started to recruit "tribal," lower-caste, and caste Hindu laborers from the Chotanagpur Plateau. Protest during that time was articulated mainly in the form of desertion, which "symbolized [the] rejection of the relationship of servitude that the emigrants were coerced into under the indentured regime. . . . It was both an individual and, sometimes, a collective act of resistance" (270). Desertion, however, had a high price for laborers when they were caught, since it was treated as a breach of contract and therefore a criminal offense punished either with fines of between Rs. 20 and 100, which was equal to five to twenty-five months' wages, or imprisonment of one to six months (270–271).

Besides desertion, other forms of resistance included shirking and cheating (e.g., plucking bad leaves in addition to good ones, hiding bricks in tea leaf baskets during weighing to fulfill their daily workload, or feigning illness to escape hard work). Another way in which laborers' resistance was articulated was through acts of violence against managers. The most violent incidents appeared as expressions of anger against physical coercion, indignities (insults, beating, etc.), or sexual exploitation of women laborers by British managers (279). Laborers killed managers in only a few cases, but many laborers were punished and imprisoned for a long time after attacking managers or threatening them with violence (280–281).

The right to impose private arrests on plantations was gradually repealed and led to a dismantling of the penal contracts in Assam in 1908. Yet, the indentured labor system continued until a spate of severe labor riots with an emphasis on economic issues happened between 1920 and 1922, on a larger scale and scope than any other labor unrest before, which Behal describes as a third phase of labor protests (287). These attacks were made against managers, on the one hand, and Indian plantation staff who had, for example, illegally deducted money from laborers' wages when paying them or taken bribes to grant them sick leave. Action was also directed toward vendors who sold their products on local markets for exorbitant prices and who were looted by laborers in revenge (287–288). Planters explained the increase in these riots by saying that the tea laborers had been influenced by Mahatma Gandhi and his noncooperation movement during the movement for independence in India, thereby denying the possibility that low wages could have caused the protests. Behal quotes tea planters, stating that "'earnings of the laborers, including concessions in the form of subsidised ration, housing, medical facilities, garden land, etc., are more than enough to maintain them in health and reasonable comfort'" (290). An inquiry committee examining the riots later, on the other hand, found it unreasonable to consider a direct link between the noncooperation movement and the riots, concluding that low wages and rising prices, together with exploitation by plantation staff and shopkeepers, were the more obvious reasons behind the protests (291). Nonetheless, the noncooperation movement and other external factors, including a successful strike by railway workers in Assam in 1920 that served tea laborers as a source of inspiration, may have had indirect influence on the labor unrest (293).

Regarding the effects of the labor revolts, Behal concludes that they were somewhat limited because laborers' demands for higher wages remained largely unfulfilled—maybe due to a lack of linkage and unity between the various incidents of protest. In comparison, the planters were united and had good connections to the government. The Workmen's Breach of Contract Act of 1859 was abolished in 1926 in line with the tea planters' protest, which Behal interprets as a successful outcome of the spate of riots in the early 1920s (294).

Since desertions were no longer illegal in the postindentured period, a new form of protest arose in what Behal calls the fourth phase of labor protest. This new form was denoted as "exodus" and meant that a mass of laborers left work and walked away. Exoduses were seen as a rejection of the "imposed rhythm of plantation life" and "extra-economic methods of exploitation," such as increased workload and delay or deductions of payments (295–296). When planters reacted to the recession in the Assam tea industry, which was caused by the Great Depression of the 1930s that had led to a decline in exports and internal consumption, by cutting wages and controlling production, laborers again reacted with protests in the form of strikes and exoduses (297).

As a kind of last phase of pre-independence protest by tea plantation laborers in Assam, Behal describes the emergence of more organized labor protest in the form of the first emerging "embryonic" labor unions between 1939 and 1947. Labor unions are discussed in detail in chapter 4.

To sum up, pre-independence labor protests on Assam tea plantations, according to Behal, were articulated as work stoppages, street protests, riots, desertions, threat and use of violence against managers, staff and vendors, exodus, and more organized labor protest when the first labor unions emerged. Behal sees the reasons for these labor protests as delayed wage payments, exploitation, increased workload, rejection of the relationship of servitude, physical coercion, indignities, and sexual exploitation of women laborers. He concludes that laborers often suffered from their engagement in protests.

Labor Protests at Work

In this section, I discuss three instances of labor protest to draw more general conclusions about laborers' underlying justice imaginaries. The first labor protest I am going to discuss falls under the category of what James Scott (1985) has called "everyday resistance." This means that an act of protest is so subtle that it could easily be overlooked as an instance of protest.[1] The incident took place in December 2016 during the pruning season. When I reached the tea plantation section where a group of laborers was supposed to be pruning that day, I heard some laborers discussing loudly with the sardar. The jamadar babu had told some laborers to work in garden number twelve that day, asking one sardar to take thirty laborers into another section at the edge of the garden to prune there. The day before, the sardar had asked thirty laborers to join him to prune that distant section of the garden. In the morning, however, around forty laborers instead of thirty had appeared, against the jamadar babu's and sardar's instructions. The sardar was afraid of getting scolded by the jamadar babu for not fulfilling his instructions, so he asked ten women to go back to garden number twelve, where they were supposed to prune. The ten laborers who had come in addition to those who had been asked to come by the sardar had appeared against the instructions given to them because they thought that the bushes would be higher in that section and therefore easier to prune than in garden number twelve. They now refused to go and started pruning the bushes against the sardar's harsh opposition. The sardar was unable to win out over the laborers' insistence to remain in this section of the garden.

This incident illustrates how laborers try to make the best out of a given situation by extending their scope of action beyond clear instructions or rules given to them by their supervisors and by challenging oppression in asymmetrical labor hierarchies. I experienced both articulations on several other occasions during my fieldwork. Other examples of the maximal extension of the scope of action can be seen in the following. Some families, for instance, made sure that one person from the household kept working on the plantation as a permanent laborer, while other family members worked elsewhere. Thereby, they could stay in the houses provided to them by the company and receive nonmonetary benefits for all the family members, while only one person provided labor to the company. Some laborers also worked for only three days a week, which was the least they needed to work in order to remain eligible for nonmonetary benefits, giving the least effort to receive the maximum return from the company. This principle could also be seen in smaller gestures, such as hiding between tea bushes during working hours to take an unnoticed small break.

The critique of labor hierarchies as expressed in the way the laborers disregarded their supervisors' instructions was also apparent on other occasions. During a picnic the management had organized for their laborers after the pruning season, for example, one laborer went to the manager, took his hand, and dragged him out to dance with the other laborers. Another incident was when a laborer working in the kitchen in the manager's bungalow laughed about the manager's wife. The wife had insulted the laborer of being careless when she felt that the temperature of her oven needed to be reduced while baking. However, the oven had only two settings: on or off. Therefore, the heat could not be reduced, and the laborer laughed at the manager's wife for not knowing the settings of her own oven that he could not have possibly changed. In all these small daily incidents, the laborers defended their position and did not accept being downgraded without criticizing labor hierarchies per se. The laborers' defense of their "dignity" was even more strongly articulated in spontaneous protests, which were more obviously seen as interruptions than the instances of "everyday resistance."

One day in December 2015 when I was chatting with Aron in his backyard, he told me about a huge fight that he had had with the plantation manager about ten years earlier. Aron had worked as a laborer on a government-owned plantation for about fifteen years when we first met in June 2015, when I incidentally ran into his wedding march. Aron's great-grandfather had come from Jharkhand to work on the plantation in the 1920s. His great-grandfather had occupied a small piece of land next to the plantation where Aron's family was still living. Aron had seven siblings. He went to school until class ten but did not take the matriculation exam because his father had died at that time. After his father's death he needed to "inherit" his father's permanent position in order to feed his family. I had visited Aron's house a couple of times before he told me about the incident that day. Aron told me that he had been working on a night shift in the plantation factory, where he and three other laborers were responsible for controlling the tea processing machinery. All three others had fallen asleep, while Aron had worked hard to look after all the machines by himself. When the manager came over to inspect the situation, he rebuked Aron for not working properly. Aron told me that he had become angry because he was the only laborer who was actually working. He remarked, "Why didn't the manager scold the ones who slept instead of me?" and continued, "I am also a human being (*insān*). I also feel sleepy at night. I also need to rest. But still I worked—me alone. Why on earth did he abuse me?" Aron recalled he then struck the manager's face out of fury. After that, the manager suspended him from work and demanded that he should beg for his pardon before reapplying for his job. Aron emphasized that he had never apologized but reapplied nonetheless a year later and was given a permanent position again. I further probed Aron about what exactly had made him so angry that day. He pointed out that "laborers should not be talked to disorderly (*ultā-pultā*) when they work properly. I am also a man (*ādmī*), a human being (*insān*), but they look at us as if we were inferior. They do not consider us to be human. What does it matter if he is the manager? I do my work and he does his work. I could not tolerate that he abused me although I did not commit a mistake (*galtī nahīn kiyā*)." Aron told me that the manager never abused him again after this incident.

Aron's spontaneous act of protest stemmed from a sense of being unjustly mistreated by the manager, as he explained. He justified his outbreak of violence by emphasizing his humanity. In doing so, he used two different Hindi terms for "human being"—*ādmī*, which can mean both "man" and "human" (or "person"), and *insān*, typically translated as "human." Another common term, *mānav*, is often used in compound phrases like "human rights" (*mānav adhikār*). Aron invoked the idea of "being human" in two distinct ways. First, he stated, "I am also a human being (*insān*). I also feel sleepy at night. I also need to rest." Here, he highlighted his physical limitations, contrasting himself with a machine that could operate continuously. Second, he used the phrase in a social and moral sense "I am also a man (*ādmī*), a human being (*insān*), but they look at us *as if* we were inferior. They do not consider us to be humans." His choice of words suggests that he rejected the notion of laborers being inferior to managers and instead held a belief in human equality. This is further evident in his rhetorical question: "What does it matter if he is the manager?"—implying that he did not see the manager's role as inherently superior to his own.

One may also read Aron's protest against the manager as a claim to "dignified work." Josh Fisher (2018) suggested the term *dignified work* as an alternative
work ethic—a mechanism by which ethical positions are formed. Fisher had conducted research with a small sewing cooperative in Nicaragua that opted out of a
free trade zone and gave up fair trade and other support to gain dignified work.
For Fisher, dignity was a recurring issue for workers in capitalist workplaces (80).
One of Fisher's interlocutors explained the meaning of dignified work as "being
recognized as people, not used as machines" (84). This is what Aron seems to
have pointed to when insisting on his shared humanity with the manager.

Moreover, Jan Philipp Reemtsma (1999) sees an idea of justice ("Gerechtigkeitsgefühl") expressed in feelings of revenge or the desire for retribution.
According to Reemtsma, the idea of justice as revenge is based on the principle
of the reciprocal infliction of suffering. When a person feels unjustly treated,
they feel as if they have become the object of another person's intentions, and
they desire revenge to equally objectify the other person to one's own desires and
thereby regain their own subjectivity.[2] Aron objectified the manager by slapping
him in order to regain his own subjectivity as a human being.

Both a violation of dignity and humiliation seemed to have also moved Rajni
and the other workers to protest as described in the incident at the beginning
of this chapter. When I walked back to the field with Rajni after the protest that
day, she showed me the uncut bushes, explaining that they had been given two
contradictory instructions by their supervisors. They were instructed to cut the
bushes a hand's width above last year's pruning mark; and they were told to prune
the bushes so that they were all at the same level. Since the laborers had not
evenly leveled them the previous year, it was impossible for the laborers to follow
both instructions. Rajni commented,

> They ask for the moon. It is impossible. The assistant manager is newly
> appointed. He came to learn things since he has no experience so far. He
> knows nothing but dared to abuse us, saying that we did not do the work
> properly (*kām ṭhīk nahīn kiyā*). If he does not know anything himself,
> how will he teach us? We work so hard (*mehanat karte hain*) and all he
> does is abuse us. He did not even tell us how to make it better. This is
> why we protested (*haḍtāl kiye*). I really do not like to be abused.

I only later came to understand the significance of the women's spontaneous
protest when Rajni told me that this was the first time they had ever done this.
When I asked her what had prompted them to protest in that way on this particular day, she kept insisting that my presence had given them courage, as the babu
(overseer) would not have dared to misbehave in my presence. Since Rajni liked
to make a lot of jokes, I was not sure if she was serious, until I mentioned it later

to the mohara, in whose house I was staying. He was astonished, saying nothing like this had ever happened to him in his section. He was even more surprised because the lower labor section was considered more "obedient" than his own.

The overseers remained silent for the rest of the day and no manager stopped by for a few days after the incident. Usually, pruning was over by twelve o'clock. That day, however, the women had only finished about two-thirds of their workload by then, due to the protest. The overseers wanted to send them home anyway, but the women insisted on finishing their workload and ended up working till half past two. When I had tea with Asha and Rajni later in the afternoon and we talked about the incident again, Asha became angry, saying,

> They always abuse us. We know that our tea estate has developed well over the last few years and makes a good profit. The manager recently got a fancy new car because the quality of the tea increased, and all we get is insults. If we do our work well, they abuse us and if we do our work bad, they abuse us even more. Today, we could not stand it any longer. The manager had abused us continuously for days; this is why we protested today. We work hard like men (*mard*). The manager will not find other women who are able to work as hard as we do.

When I asked Asha a few days later whether she thought that anything had changed after the protest, she replied, with a beaming smile,

> Yes, nobody has abused us, and we did not see the manager again. No one disturbs us anymore. See, we have to live here for all our life. We cannot go elsewhere. You will leave again in a few months. The managers stay here for a few years before they move on elsewhere. But we always have to live here, that is why the work needs to be all right for us. The managers talk too much, "this is not right, that is not right . . ." but they know nothing. The laborers on this plantation are very good but the managers still abuse us. This is not right (*ṭhīk nahīn hain*). We are a lot of laborers together. We could do anything. On other plantations, laborers kill managers. But the laborers on our plantation are all right. They would never do something like that. Still, they abuse us. This is just not right (*ṭhīk nahīn hain*).

Different conclusions can be drawn from this incident of spontaneous protest regarding laborers' conceptions of justice. The laborers temporarily refused to work, staging a sit-down strike. For some time, they did not obey their supervisors' verbal and physical instructions to get back to work, resisting their demands by deciding to remain seated and emphasizing verbally that they were not going back to work. Their bodies, which they usually utilized as a means of labor, became a means of protest for them through their refusal to move and work. The laborers asserted that they had chosen this type of protest for the first time in their lives. They could have chosen different means of protest instead. For example, they could have decided to protest in a more radical way, such as using violence against the managers or overseers, as Aron had. They could also have decided to protest in a more subtle way, such as cutting the remaining bushes even worse, which could have gone unnoticed, as a way of "everyday protest." However, they decided on a middle course by protesting noticeably but moderately.

Possibly the laborers did not opt for a more radical form of protest because they were afraid of the severe consequences such a radical protest might have had for them. The laborers on Dolani Tea Estate had once surrounded the manager's office in the plantation factory and threatened to attack the manager if he did not pay them their annual bonus, which he had not fully done so far that year. The manager had somehow managed to flee from his office. I did not observe this incident, which happened some ten years before I conducted my fieldwork, but different laborers told me about it and its dramatic turn several times. The manager never returned to the plantation and was probably moved to manage another one of his company's plantations. However, the factory and the plantation remained closed for about two weeks afterward. The laborers could not work and received no payment before the plantation was eventually reopened by a new manager. The older laborers who had participated in the protest remembered it as a traumatic event, since they had almost starved in the absence of pay and food rations when the company closed the plantation down. In the end, their protest had had more negative consequences for them than for the manager or the company. I assume that this kind of negative experience of more radical forms of protest, which was frequently recalled in conversations among laborers, held them back, on the day I described above, from taking more drastic measures. Being women may have also contributed to their hesitation to protest more violently as Aron had done, which points to the gendered differences in options for resistance.

The laborers did not opt for more subtle ways of everyday protest either but wanted to protest in a visible way. They said that they had decided to protest in a more obvious way because they had been unjustifiably abused by an inexperienced and incompetent manager, who did not know how to do things better. They evaluated his abuse as unjustified because their work outcome deficiency was not the result of their lack of effort or hard work but the result of instructions that were impossible to put into action. Later, Asha put forward two additional explanations for their protest action. The first was that, considering that the plantation was making a good profit, it was not fair for the manager to be rewarded with a new car while the laborers got insults although the company's profit resulted from their hard labor. Behind this argument is an idea of distributive justice that rewards the ones working hard. Asha did not specify what kind of reward she was thinking of, but from her utterance one can assume that she meant both material and nonmaterial rewards—material rewards because she mentioned the manager's new car, which he received as a reward, and nonmaterial rewards because she indirectly mentioned the opposite of being rewarded with insults, which is acknowledgment. The second argument that Asha provided was that laborers had to live on the plantations for the rest of their lives, unlike managers (or anthropologists), which is why she saw a need to engage in keeping labor relations and conditions bearable for them.

From the protesting laborers' reasoning for why they had protested that day, it is possible to draw more general conclusions about how they envisioned just labor conditions and relations, and about their work ethos (Eckert 2020, 11). The laborers' most obvious complaint was about being abused despite having worked as hard and as diligently as they could. This reasoning resembles Aron's work ethos described above. The laborers also found it unjustifiable to be abused when they had not done anything wrong. Eventually, the laborers won their case that day, which can be seen from the immediate effects of their protest. The overseers remained silent for the rest of the day, the manager did not show up for a couple of days, and the overseers wanted to send the women home although they had not fulfilled their daily target by twelve o'clock. These reactions may be interpreted either as an indirect admission of guilt on behalf of the overseers or as a sign that the overseers were afraid that this kind of protest may happen again or turn into something bigger.

Another striking aspect of that day's events was that the workers insisted on completing their daily workload, even when their supervisors wanted to send them home. Despite having to work two-and-a-half hours of overtime, they remained determined. I assume they wanted to assert that they were the ones working properly, upholding their work ethos even after being unjustly mistreated. By refusing to accept a favor from their supervisors, they reclaimed their dignity and corrected a perceived wrong.

Laborers on Dolani Tea Estate seldom participated in more organized protests. They explained to me that they sometimes wanted to participate in organized protests but could not afford to, since they would have to pay for public transport in order to reach the protest site, which amounted to about a week's income of a normal plantation laborer and meant incurring an additional loss of money through absence from work. Therefore, when I participated in public protests on behalf of tea plantation laborers, I found that most protesters were either representatives of activist groups (discussed in more detail in chap. 4) or better-educated children of tea plantation workers. Once, in March 2015, I participated in a protest in front of the trade unions central office in Dibrugarh after the trade union had signed a wage agreement below the statutory minimum wage. About one thousand people had come to join the protest from various places in Assam. Directly in front of the gate of the trade union's office, people were delivering speeches in Sadri. In front of me, a group of women held up protest posters with Sadri inscriptions in Assamese script. I asked the women about what was written on their posters to start a conversation. One woman disclosed that they could not read or write, so they did not know exactly what was written on their poster. They told me that some activists who had organized the protest had given them the posters to hold up. One woman explained that they had come because they wanted more money. When I asked them how much money they were claiming, the women looked at each other queryingly for a while. Another male protestor who stood beside us said to both the women and I that they had come to claim the minimum wage of Rs. 169. I further asked the women why they were claiming more money. One answered, "We cannot make a living from what we earn (*is paise se ghar nahin cālā sakte hain*). We have to eat, educate our children, buy clothes and other things, therefore we need a little more money." Another woman explained, "We work so hard, and we get so little money. That is not right." Another male laborer from a neighboring district told me, "I have come to protest (*dharnā*). We do (hard) manual labor (*mazdūr kā kām*) but earn so little money. The money is not sufficient (*santuṣṭ*). We cannot make a living from it (*ghar nahin cālā sakte hain*). Besides, the government declared 169. Prices are also increasing. We need Rs. 330 to make a living (*jīvan bitāne ke lie*)."

This showed the protestors' different levels of engagement with the topic of the protest. Some protestors were uninformed about the details of the wage agreement and the protest organizers' official claims. They had simply come because they wanted "more money."

Some may not even have known what the protest was about before reaching the protest site, which I experienced on another occasion, when I was asked to join a group of women at a protest in a district capital. When I tried to find out what the protest would be about, I got vague and contradictory answers related to improving the tea plantation laborers' situation. I decided to join the protest. When we reached the district capital where the protest was to take place, we jumped out of the car that had been provided by the protest organizers. Protest posters were pressed into our hands, similar to the women protesting in front of the trade union office that other day, and we directly joined the protest march that had just started when we arrived without knowing what was written on the protest posters we were holding. Later, I came to know it was a demonstration about the rights of people with disabilities on World Disability Day. When I asked the organizing NGO people why they had decided to call tea plantation laborers to join their protest, they explained that it was because many people with disabilities lived on tea plantations. For the women it turned out to be a nice outing paid for by the NGO, and for the NGO, the women laborers constituted a good crowd of people to demonstrate the importance of their protest's issues. This illustrates that people may join a protest for very different reasons, which do not necessarily agree with those of the organizer. However, during the protest, participants may become aware of the organizers' goals and leave with a new or broadened understanding of their objectives.

Moreover, even if protestors were participating in a demonstration for similar reasons to those intended by the organizers, they may have different interpretations of the protest's objectives. In the first case outlined above, while some protestors had come to claim an indefinite amount of "more money" because they believed they were not able to make a living from the wages they earned, others brought forward a more concrete claim for "just" wages in terms of the statutory minimum wage or a living wage. In the first case, the tea planters were addressed as responsible agents of justice to provide "more money." In the other case, the state is also addressed to implement minimum wages for tea plantation laborers. The most commonly articulated reason why the protestors were claiming higher wages was that prices were increasing, and their wages were no longer sufficient to live on—an argument that is as old as the tea industry itself, according to what the historian Rana Behal has written about early forms of labor protests during the colonial period. Behind that lies a subsistence ethic—a belief that wages need to be high enough to secure subsistence. Another argument was that wages were not "appropriate" for the hard manual work that laborers did for the tea companies.

Justice in Context

This chapter takes the argument by James Scott (1976, 158) that injustice can only be perceived if people have a norm of justice in mind from which it has departed as a starting point to understand tea plantation laborers' justice imaginaries through different forms of protest motivated by feelings of experienced injustice that reveal underlying norms of justice. In everyday forms of protest, laborers sought to rectify labor hierarchies and move immediate superiors to give them what they consider to be due to them. Aron's violent protest against his manager and the women laborers' sit-down strike both happened when they felt falsely accused of not working properly while actually upholding the work ethos in a remarkable way. Protests occurred primarily when laborers sought respect and acknowledgment for their hard work in nonmonetary terms. This is supported by tea laborers' loyalty toward the tea companies described in the previous chapter and their holding on to nonmonetary benefits as illustrated in the anecdote at the beginning of the introduction to this book. When I started my fieldwork in December 2014, there were rumors that tea plantation laborers' food rations would be abandoned because companies were hesitant to provide them since laborers were also eligible for subsidized food rations under the Indian state's public distribution system. The rumors caused lively debates on plantations about the possibility of no longer receiving food rations. Laborers articulated that it would be the worst-case scenario for them if food rations or the dual-wage structure were to be abandoned.

Tea plantation laborers as both concerned agents of justice and subjects of justice considered provisions prescribed in the Plantations Labour Act and respect and acknowledgment for their hard work (as objects of justice) to be due to them by tea planters and sometimes the state as responsible agents of justice. In making this statement about what workers believed they were entitled to, I do not mean to suggest that they felt no dissatisfaction with the old-style plantation economy, nor that they lacked aspirations beyond it. Many workers, like Manoj (see chap. 1), dreamed of a life of freedom as subsistence farmers outside the plantations. Others, like Jiya's husband, hoped for better-paying jobs away from the plantations (see chap. 2). Many workers simply wanted their children to receive a good education and secure better jobs outside the plantations, as others have similarly expressed (e.g., Besky 2014; Jegathesan 2019). Some workers aspired to own items like motorcycles for prestige. When I last saw Rajni in 2023, she proudly showed me the scooter she had long desired and finally managed to buy for herself. I am not suggesting that workers were uncritical of the plantation economy or lacked dreams beyond it. They had a wide range of aspirations. However, since my primary concern here is with notions of justice—specifically how workers' ideas of justice relate to the visions of advocacy groups aiming to bring justice closer to laborers—my focus is on what laborers considered to be their due. This was not an expensive car or anything comparable, but rather recognition for their hard work and entitlements like food rations, as prescribed by the Plantations Labour Act. Asha, in her earlier statement, did not claim she was entitled to a luxury car like the manager's; rather, she believed she deserved to be appreciated for her labor.

I argue that this idea is far from naive or unrevolutionary. On the contrary, striving to rectify labor regulations and relations based on the old-style political economy of tea production can bring about transformations within the existing system, as long as it remains intact. However, in a historical moment when these structures are being disrupted and possibly dismantled, as detailed in the introduction, adhering to an old-style political economy based on the Plantations Labour Act becomes more revolutionary than reformative. Theoretically, this means that if the same justice framework is applied in a new context, it can shift from preserving existing structures to undermining them, or vice versa.

JUSTICE AND CATEGORIES OF COLLECTIVE IDENTIFICATION

One morning in March 2015, during my fieldwork in Assam, I woke up to a call from an Adivasi activist telling me that there was going to be a demonstration in one of Assam's district capitals that day. On the spur of the moment, I rushed out and took a bus to the city where the protest was supposed to be taking place. Reaching the spot, I saw about a hundred people gathering. Augustin, an activist I knew from before, recognized me and slipped out of the crowd to great me. He was wearing a dark red Adivasi *gamchā* (cotton towel) wrapped around his head. I asked Augustin what the protest was about. "One sixty-nine," he replied, referring to the statutory minimum wage at that time, which was Rs. 169. The trade union had just agreed to a wage hike that was below this statutory minimum wage, and the Adivasi activists were there to protest this "illegal" wage agreement. The protestors shouted slogans loudly and synchronously: "*ACMS murdabad!*" ("Down with the trade union!") They shouted one slogan in English: "No justice—no rest!"

What conception of justice was in the minds of the protestors when they shouted, "No justice—no rest," and in the minds of the trade unionists when they signed the "illegal" wage agreement? At the time I was conducting my fieldwork, the trade union argued that agreeing to wages below the statutory minimum level was acceptable because nonmonetary benefits made up the difference. Adivasi activists had previously mainly promoted affirmative action as a means to improve the livelihoods of Adivasi tea laborers in Assam, but they started demanding minimum wages on plantations in 2014 under the guidance of international NGOs.

In this chapter, I focus on how changing conceptions of justice work at categories of collective identification by analyzing the different ways in which Assam tea plantation laborers are represented by different kinds of activists. While the literature on Indian tea plantations has focused on the "persistent association between ethnicity, place, and work" (Besky 2017a, 619; see also Raj 2013), I discuss the fuzziness and flexibility of tea laborers' collective categories of identification and their sociopolitical implications. I use the term *categories of identification* rather than *collective identities* to highlight the processual, contingent, and versatile character of identity (see Eidson et al. 2017).

I argue that changing visions of justice have transformed Assam tea laborers' categories of collective identification, turning them from "tea tribes" into Adivasis, and further into subjects of labor rights. As all these categories of collective identification are still actively used in Assam, the transformation should not be understood as linear and consecutive but as parallel and entangled. Tea plantation laborers in Assam have been, and still are, commonly designated as "tea tribes" or "ex–tea tribes" (those who no longer work on the plantation but still reside in villages adjacent to the plantations). Although the term *tribal* does not necessarily have "pejorative connotations" in India (Karlsson and Subba 2006, 4; Xaxa 2014), during my fieldwork Adivasi activists felt discriminated against because of the designation "tea tribes" and preferred to use the term *Adivasi* to describe both current and former tea laborers in Assam generally.[1] Adivasi movements in other parts of India have received broad scholarly attention (e.g., Nilsen 2012; Sanchez and Strümpell 2014; Shah 2010; Steur 2014). Studying Adivasis in Assam is particularly interesting because Adivasi groups are not recognized as Scheduled Tribes in Assam as they are in other Indian states, and Scheduled Tribes in Assam do not consider themselves as being Adivasis. This complicates the common equation of Adivasis with Scheduled Tribes and related questions of collective identification.

Since most of Assam's tea plantation laborers are Adivasis, the terms *tea laborers*, *Adivasis*, and *tea tribes* are often used interchangeably. Because these categories of identification seem broadly overlapping, replacing one collective designation with another appears to be only a matter of political correctness. However, I argue that the discrepancy between seemingly identical categories of identification and their specific situational adaptations in struggles for justice works along leadership patterns among activists. In this chapter, I discuss different justice imaginaries promoted by trade unionists, Adivasi activists and international labor activists, analyzing how they each influence laborers' categories of identification and how these in turn affect leadership patterns. As highlighted in the introduction, the analyzed justice imaginaries are not immutable, clear-cut, and unambiguous but rather serve as heuristic devices to understand what people consider to be due to them and others.

Trade Unionists and the "Old-Style" Tea Plantation Economy

The Indian Trade Union Movement in India started in the 1920s with the establishment of the All India Trade Union Congress (AITUC) as the first national trade union in India (Ali 2011, 33). The first semblances of trade union–type organizations for tea laborers on plantations in Assam emerged in the late 1930s, at a time when a "fierce outburst of labor struggles all over the province of Assam" appeared in various industries, such as oil or railways (Behal 2014, 300). The first attempts to create union-like organizations on tea plantations were conducted by Congress Party members who tried to intervene as mediators in conflicts between planters and laborers. They were, however, not accepted by planters and could therefore not gain any substantial influence at that time. In 1939, other non-plantation industries in Assam had formed the first labor unions—for example, Digboi oil workers—which inspired the idea of a stronger labor unionization on plantations (301). P. M. Sarwan, a Christian who grew up on a tea plantation in Assam, formed the Chota Nagpuri Association in 1938, which aimed to improve tea plantation laborers' welfare under the influence of Christian missionaries from Central India (302). Historical sources mention four labor unions for tea laborers that formed as early as 1939 in the Assam Valley. Yet not much is known about these early unions' activities, which is why Rana Behal concludes that "it is likely that they never really became very effective" (302–303). Behal assumes that the reason behind the limited influence of these early trade union formations may be seen in the context of World War II, when the Indian government justified crushing labor unions in the name of defense under the Defense of India Rules, which allowed draconian measures against many forms of protest (303). A decline of labor unrest due to these strict political restrictions went on well into the early 1940s, although the harsh decline in real wages due to increased prices during wartime caused new resentment among tea laborers (303).

The Assam branch of AITUC, called Assam Provincial Trade Union Congress (APTUC), was formed in 1943 as the first labor organization at the province level in Assam (303). During APTUC's first state-level conference in Dibrugarh in 1943, its communist leaders raised progressive demands for tea laborers in Assam, including the following: a daily minimum wage of Rs. 1 for men and women alike; no increase in workload when wages increased; the abolition of child labor; an appropriate amount and quality of food rations and clothes at subsidized rates for laborers' families; the provision of clean drinking water; fortified houses and latrines; free compulsory primary education; a tripartite committee of trade unions, planters, and government representatives to discuss tea laborers' economic, social, and political conditions; and the granting of civil rights (e.g., freedom of assembly) to laborers (304).

Encouraged by the communist union and its claims, tea laborers engaged in a new wave of labor protests, which were at times brutally defeated by the planters. For instance, there was a protest in which all laborers stopped working for two days and assembled in front of a manager's office. The manager killed one protestor, ran away, and was never sentenced for the murder. This incident caused the first collaboration between tea workers and workers from other industries against their common experience of exploitation; subsequently, the Assam Chah-Bagan Mazdoor Union was founded by communist activists (305). However, tea plantation laborers' "struggles did not emerge into a united labor organization which could involve the entire labor force working in the Assam Valley tea plantations till the end of colonial rule" (306) when the Congress Party's trade union wing, the Indian National Trade Union Congress (INTUC), the second-largest of five present-day recognized Central Trade Union Organizations in India, gained monopoly over the organization of plantation labor in the tea industry in Assam (J. Sharma 2011, 235). In contrast to APTUC, INTUC was supported and patronized by tea planters and was supported by the first postindependence elected Congress government in India on the national level and in Assam on the state level (Behal 2014, 305).

Tea planters in Assam had generally opposed the setting up of trade unions for tea plantation laborers until the early 1940s by arguing that "outsiders" were seeking to exploit "illiterate" laborers for political reasons (307). However, according to Rana Behal, toward the mid-1940s planters realized that they could no longer uphold their total opposition because trade unions had become more common and influential. Accordingly, they changed their strategy toward accepting only trade unions "which were willing to accept their terms and conditions" (308).

During my research, the Assam Tea Workers' Union (Assam Chah Mazdoor Sangha or ACMS), established in 1957, was the single most important trade union for tea plantation laborers in Assam.[2] It is affiliated to INTUC. Until 2014, the ACMS negotiated wage increases for tea plantation laborers in the Assam Valley bilaterally with the Consultative Committee of Plantation Associations (CCPA), a tea planters' union. The ACMS covers all plantations in the Assam Valley and has approximately 350,000 members. It has more than three hundred employees, and initially leadership positions were held primarily by "caste Hindu middle-class men from outside the labor communities," which is characteristic of the Indian trade union movement in general (J. Sharma 2011, 235). Over time, however, the ACMS developed "an 'insider' union élite," meaning that the laborers themselves, or former laborers, or laborers' children, can now gain leadership positions. Lower-level leadership positions on the plantation are often occupied by laborers, while higher leadership positions are usually taken by their children. ACMS leaders are mainly caste Hindus today, such as Tanti, Karamkar, and Gwala, some of whom are categorized as Other Backward Classes (OBC) in Assam.[3]

When I visited the ACMS head office in Dibrugarh in 2015, I asked the general secretary, Dileshwar Tanti, why he had voted against implementing the statutory minimum wage of Rs. 169 during the last wage negotiations. His phone rang at that precise moment, and while he took the call, an administrative staffer sitting next to us exclaimed, "But the minimum wage is implemented if you take non-monetary benefits into account!" When Tanti finished his call, he added, "I voted for Rs. 115. One sixty-nine has no basis because the industries are so different, and in the tea industry there are many other obligations that are not there in other industries." He then explained that he believed Rs. 115 constituted a "fair" wage because "one fifteen with benefits is sufficient, and it is also within the management's capacity to pay" —that is, it would not cause the whole industry to collapse.[4]

FIGURE 10.   ACMS logo on a picture in Dileshwar Tanti's office. Photo by the author, Assam 2015.

The ACMS's aim of maintaining the "old-style" tea plantation economy by promoting wages that are "within the industry's capacity to pay" must be contextualized within the Indian tea industry's recent economic and legal transformations as described in the introduction, which are characterized by, among other things, a gradual disarticulation of Assam tea production from the capitalist world economy; a shift from a plantation-dominated industry to a gradual replacement of plantations with smallholdings; a shift from the standard of permanent labor contracts to a casualization of labor; and the replacement of welfare labor laws with a new labor law regime that dismantles labor laws characterized by extensive social welfare measures. Hence, the trade union tried to retain the "old-style" plantation economy when it started being replaced by a new, less regulated political economy of Assam tea production. This is similar to the argument by E. P. Thompson (1971) that "the crowd" in eighteenth-century England was influenced by a "moral economy"—a specific social field of thought and action in which older, paternalistic practices and normative ideas were confronted with the practices and normative ideas of a "new political economy." Assam trade unionists were similarly attached to the normative ideas of the old-style moral economy of tea production based on comprehensive welfare measures legally prescribed in the Plantations Labour Act (PLA).

In the context of economic and legal transformation in India's tea plantation economy, the ACMS trade union opposed certain labor rights, such as the introduction of statutory minimum wages, in order to maintain an old-style plantation economy that provided dependent but secure livelihoods to tea plantation laborers. Adivasi activists, by contrast, based their justice imaginaries for tea workers on them receiving unconditional legal entitlements.

Adivasi Activists Fighting for Affirmative Action

The Adivasi movement in Assam evolved in the 1990s and consists of several organizations. The first organization, founded by Adivasi activists in 1996, is a student association called All Adivasi Students' Association of Assam (AASAA). In the early 2000s, additional NGOs were established—for example, People's Action for Development. Lastly, Adivasi activists registered a trade union in 2016 called Assam Mazdoor Union, which has not yet gained much influence. Adivasi activists are mainly the children or grandchildren of tea plantation laborers or former laborers. I will discuss the development and constitution of the Adivasi movement in Assam further below and focus for now on one of the Adivasi movement's most important justice imaginaries: to gain recognition for Adivasis as Scheduled Tribes in Assam, as they are recognized as such in most other Indian federal states, to render them eligible for affirmative action in Assam.[5] One Adivasi magazine states the centrality of this aim for the Adivasi movement, which I encountered many times during my fieldwork: "Adivasi organizations . . . point to a particular policy feature that is historically missing here in Assam, which is the granting of Scheduled Tribe (ST) status to the Adivasis. . . . It is often the central, if not only, point of many of their campaigns" (Nawa Bihan Samaj 2013, 35).

Most Adivasis living in Assam are either current or former tea plantation laborers or their descendants. Adivasi activists' conviction that Adivasis deserve

FIGURE 11.   Cover of bimonthly Adivasi news magazine. Photo by the author, Assam 2017.

preferential treatment as Scheduled Tribes in Assam is based partly on their claim that they constitute India's "original inhabitants" and partly on their status as Scheduled Tribes in other Indian federal states. For instance, one Adivasi activist commented, "Juel Oram [a BJP politician from the Indian state of Odisha] is a tribal himself. How can he be a tribal and I am not—we have the same surname. How can I be OBC?" The argument evokes the larger idea of justice as the equal treatment of equals and takes the Indian nation-state instead of Indian federal states as the reference scale of justice. The main reasons cited for not recognizing Adivasis as Scheduled Tribes in Assam are that they are not indigenous to Assam and because of "inter-tribe contestation" (Ananthanarayanan 2010; Sharma and Khan 2018, 202). Townsend Middleton (2013, 15), in his study of civil servants who verify India's Scheduled Tribes, shows that there is "no standardized procedure for certifying 'tribal' communities." He states that "the viability of ST status derives not only from the advantages that the designation offers, but also from the pliability of the 'tribal' category itself" (13).

This lack of standardization contributes to confusion about the relationship between indigeneity and "backwardness" in granting ST status.[6] Along with Adivasis, five other groups in Assam currently claim ST status; among them are Thai-Ahom and Koch-Rajbonshi, historically the ruling classes in Assam. Thai-Ahom and Koch-Rajbonshi justify their claim by highlighting their indigeneity to the region and by disregarding their historically privileged socioeconomic status. The fact that Adivasis are only one group among others claiming ST status in Assam is seen as one major reason why they have not yet been acknowledged as ST in Assam. On the one hand, there is a fear of political unrest if only one community among those demanding recognition is acknowledged as a Scheduled Tribe. On the other hand, it is feared that (parts of) Assam may turn into a "tribal area." According to the Indian constitution's Sixth Schedule, regions with a "tribal" majority can turn into semiautonomous "tribal areas" with "tribal" political institutions (Middleton 2013, 14).

Since indigenous populations have often been discriminated against, historical discrimination and indigeneity are commonly linked (Zenker 2022). However, indigeneity is, to an extent, decoupled from historical discrimination in Assam, and therefore it has become possible for Assam's historical aristocracy to claim ST status based on the idea that its members, as the firstcomers to the region, are entitled to certain privileges (see Béteille 1998). If all six communities come to be recognized as Scheduled Tribes in Assam, it will be hard for Adivasis to compete with people from a historically privileged aristocratic class. Frustrated by the continuous denial of ST status, in 2014 Adivasi activists started giving more attention to labor rights, or more precisely to the drive for a statutory minimum wage for tea plantation laborers.

The Campaign for Statutory Minimum Wages

The International Labour Organization (2017, 4) defines a minimum wage as "the minimum amount of remuneration that an employer is required to pay wage earners for the work performed during a given period, which cannot be reduced by collective agreement or an individual contract." Minimum wages were first fixed in New Zealand and Australia in the late nineteenth century and were defined for particular regions and fields of labor, mainly low-wage labor (Starr 1981). The first international law to promote minimum wages was implemented by the organization's *Minimum Wage Fixing Machinery Convention* of 1928. Minimum wages in India were introduced through the Minimum Wages Act of 1948.

Adivasi activists in Assam learned about the minimum wage and the living wage in India from two international NGOs that conducted legal capacity trainings for leading Adivasi activists in July 2014, just before the wage negotiations began.[7] Following the training, Adivasi activists started a wage campaign for tea laborers in Assam. The shift from affirmative action to labor law also means that tea plantation issues are now considered more explicitly in the Adivasi movement. One Adivasi activist stated, "Initially, we did not focus so much on tea gardens. We rather fought for our community's right to get the ST status. The wage campaign was the first big initiative on tea gardens."

Some weeks after the protest against the wage agreement described at the beginning of this chapter, in which the trade union consented to a wage below the statutory minimum wage, I visited Mark, a prominent Adivasi activist who had led the protest that day (see fig. 12). We met in his house on a tea plantation. Mark was the son of tea pluckers; although his father had died some years earlier, his mother still plucked tea. Mark had decided to join the Adivasi movement when he was still in school, after seeing media reports about the first large protest of the Adivasi movement in Guwahati, the capital of Assam.

During that protest, civilians and police officers had beaten up protesters and had stripped a woman protester naked and harassed her. When Mark saw that "our people are treated like animals," it became a turning point in his life, he said. Mark became agitated as he spoke, raking his fingers through his moustache. Mark explained why he thought the trade union should not have agreed to the "illegal" wage agreement: "It is stated in our constitution . . . that the minimum wage for tea laborers should be Rs. 169. The reason for our movement (*āndolan*) is that we should get Rs. 169. . . . We live in a democracy. . . . It is our right (*adhikār*) to make demands! Our calculation is that one person (*ādmī*) needs at least Rs. 330 per day to live on (*ghar cālāne ke lie*). But the lowest wage should not be below the minimum wage!"

FIGURE 12.   Protest in front of the trade union's head office in Dibrugarh. Photo by the author, Assam 2015.

Mark's statement illustrates how Adivasi activists applied their newly acquired knowledge about the statutory minimum wage in their movement. Mark called the wage agreement "illegal" because he considers the minimum wage to be a constitutional right; he sees laborers as being entitled to a minimum wage because they are citizens of India endowed with certain (labor) rights. Mark's and the Adivasi movement's claim appears in a broader context when "citizenship has resurfaced as a central format of struggles for justice and social well-being" (Eckert 2011, 309). Thereby, Mark, like other Adivasi activists, demands the unconditional fulfillment of Indian labor law for tea plantation laborers as Indian citizens, regardless of the tea industry's capacity to pay.

The wage of Rs. 330 per day that Mark is seeking had been suggested by the international NGOs as a "just wage" —a wage that would enable tea laborers to cover their basic expenses like clothing and food as well as additional costs like housing, electricity, education, medical care, and an old-age pension. The proposed "just wage," which activists sometimes also referred to as a "living wage," starts from a needs-based minimum wage. Needs-based minimum wages were drawn up by the Tripartite Committee of the 15th Indian Labour Conference in 1957, which declared that minimum wages in India should be calculated to ensure "minimum human needs" (Ministry of Labour and Employment 2008).

Since the current Indian labor law reform and the replacement of the Plantations Labour Act with the Code on Occupational Safety, Health and Working Conditions is ongoing, it is unclear whether nonmonetary benefits will continue to be paid next to higher cash wages in the Indian tea industry or if higher cash wages will eventually replace the dual wage structure. There is a lack of agreement about whether higher cash wages in the Indian tea industry have primarily positive or negative implications. Some people regard the elimination of non-monetary compensation in the Indian tea industry as "a welcome decolonization of agriculture," while others fear consequences such as the "breakup of both families and social and ethical lifeworlds" (Besky 2017a, 628).

On February 26, 2015, the trade union, the ACMS, and the planter's union, the CCPA, came up with a decision to increase wages from Rs. 94 to Rs. 115 that was below the statutory minimum wage of Rs. 169 and far below the requested living wage of Rs. 330. The wage increase was nonetheless historically high. Until 2014, tea plantation laborers' wages in Assam had been increased by just a few rupees per year; after, the increases became bigger, and since 2023, laborers have earned Rs. 250 per day.[8]

The implications of the higher cash wages and the possible erasure of non-monetary benefits in the tea industry must be studied carefully in the future. But in this chapter, I want to focus on an aspect that has received little attention in the ongoing debate: how shifting visions of justice shape tea laborers' categories of identification and the sociopolitical consequences that arise from this.

Situational Adaptations of Collective Identities

The shared labor migration history of tea plantation laborers from the "tribal belt" led to their labeling as "tea tribes" in Assam, while those who migrated to the villages surrounding the tea plantations in Assam are called "ex–tea tribes." This category gained limited official status when "Tea Garden and Ex-Tea Garden Tribes" were mentioned in a 1946 memorandum of the Assam government, which defines ex–tea garden tribes as "descendants of 'immigrants who originally came for employment in tea garden'" (Kikon 2017, 320). The term *tea tribes* appears in official administrative designations such as the Assam government's "Tea Tribes and Adivasi Welfare Department" or by the denotation of the first interest group for tea laborers, the All Assam Tea Tribes Student Association (ATTSA). The group is closely linked to the trade union, ACMS. However, the

term *tea tribe* does not have the same legal meaning as collective ethnic designations, such as "Munda" and "Oraon," which may be declared "tribes" eligible
for affirmative action. The notion "tea tribes" also resembles the local notions
bāgāniyā or *bāgān ke log*, which can be literally translated as "garden people."

While the terms *tea tribes* and *ex-tea tribes* are commonly used, Adivasi
activists have resisted being designated as such because they feel the terms are
derogatory—not because of the term *tribe* but because of its combination with
tea. Adivasi activists often asked me rhetorically: "How can a tribe be named
after a commodity?" The Adivasi movement has struggled to replace the term
tea tribe with *Adivasi* and to encourage tea laborers to identify as Adivasi rather
than with their particular ethnic group. For example, an Adivasi activist from the
Khondo community on a tea plantation in Assam commented, "I do not know
what is particular about Khondos. We do not have a Khondo society or common Khondo celebrations [as other ethnic groups have]. . . . But I am also not
interested in preserving the Khondo culture. My sentiment goes toward being
Adivasi. If everyone focuses too much on his own separate *jāti*, then there will be
a divide, and our Adivasi community will become weak."

The terminological shift from "tea tribes" or from the names of their constituent ethnic groups (*jātis*) to "Adivasis" has been an implicit objective of the Adivasi movement from its outset. The common narrative told by Adivasi activists
traces the movement's inception back to 1996. In that year, about 250 Adivasis
were killed by Bodo extremists in plantations and villages in Lower Assam (West
Assam), and more than 200,000 people were expelled from their homes without
being properly resettled (Bora 2014). The Bodos are the largest Scheduled Tribe
in Assam. Bodo extremists attacked Adivasis because Adivasis do not support
their claim for an independent state, Bodoland, and because the Bodos oppose
Adivasis' claim to ST status due to intertribe contestation. Adivasi activists assert
that neither the government nor any of the existing interest groups took care of
Adivasi victims after the Bodo attack, which is why they decided to form their
own movement. One of the Adivasi movement's founders, who was a teacher at
that time, recalled the experience of ethnic violence toward Adivasis in 1996 and
how this became a turning point in his life:

> In 1996, an ethnic attack took place in Kokrajhar [district in Lower
> Assam]. It was an ethnic clash between Bodo and Adivasi. When I saw it
> on TV, my mind was very disturbed. And without permission from my
> school, I went to Kokrajhar and stayed there for some days. . . . There
> were thousands of people sleeping on the open roads at night. And it was
> very painful to see the situation. Because of that scenery, I myself ques-
> tioned many things, and it was a turning point of my life. Many people

say that this was a turning point for the Adivasi society. . . . I resigned from school. . . . I was present at that meeting where AASAA [All Adivasi Students' Association of Assam, the first organization that was established by Adivasi activists on July 2, 1996] was founded. At that time, we were trying to build AASAA to unite our community so that we could fight for our rights. I completely gave up teaching and engaged in building up that organization. . . . We were forced to form an organization to protest against all this injustice to the Adivasi community.

Former organizations working for the welfare of the "tea tribes," such as the All Assam Tea Tribes Students' Association (ATTSA), commentated critically on the emergence of new interest groups. Ajay, an ATTSA district-level president, remarked, "Nowadays, different organizations have been formed. Before, there were only two organizations [the trade union and ATTSA]. We were working from one platform. What I want to say is that the unity or strength that was there before got weakened." Ajay said this as an Odia caste Hindu, the group that occupies most leadership positions in both ATTSA and the trade union ACMS. Ajay bewails the fact that unity has been disturbed by the emergence of new interest groups. However, although all the "tea tribes" are included as ATTSA's protégés, only certain people have been able to gain leadership positions in ATTSA and ACMS alike—namely, (male) caste Hindus.

Therefore, an Adivasi activist once suggested another reason why it was important to form an Adivasi movement in Assam. Caste Hindus like the Odia often considered Adivasis to be inferior. Thus, Adivasis formed their own movement to provide social upward mobility opportunities for their Adivasi leaders, since they would only give leadership positions to Adivasis.

As the Adivasi movement has gained in popularity, the fuzziness of categories of identification in the emergence of new interest groups with different visions of justice has caused leadership patterns to change. This is a dynamic that is often overlooked in the public debate on Adivasi claims to be recognized as Scheduled Tribes in Assam.

First, it must be kept in mind that the term *Adivasi* has no legal recognition in India today (Parmar 2016, 6). Although *Adivasi* is an umbrella term designating diverse ethnic groups, it would not be legally possible to acknowledge Adivasis as Scheduled Tribes in Assam. Of the estimated ninety-six "tribes" who work as laborers on tea plantations in Assam, only twenty-six are listed as Scheduled Tribes elsewhere in India and could therefore be considered for possible designation as Scheduled Tribes in Assam as well (Choudhury 2015).

Second, while Adivasi activists used the terms *tea tribes, tea plantation laborers,* and *Adivasis* synonymously in the "public transcript," they differentiated between "real" and "false" Adivasis in the "hidden transcript" (Scott 1990). Only "real" Adivasis, meaning those who had been acknowledged as Scheduled Tribes in other Indian states, were allowed to take leading positions in the Adivasi movement, even though the Adivasi movement claimed to represent all Adivasis or all tea plantation laborers (and ex–tea laborers) in Assam. Adivasi activists were playing with the alignment of different ethnic groups under the umbrella term *Adivasi* in different situations and for different purposes (Eidson et al. 2017, 341). This public inclusion and internal exclusion of "false" Adivasis resembles the way ATTSA and ACMS open up leadership positions to caste Hindus alone, despite claiming to speak on behalf of all tea laborers.

Hence, many people wanted to join the most powerful movement. One Odia said,

> Actually, I am also confused myself about what Adivasi means. Maybe I can say that personally I am Oriya, but in order to access governmental schemes, I have to call myself Adivasi.[9] Formerly, we were tea tribes and there was a Tea and Ex-Tea Tribes Board to access governmental schemes. Now the Adivasi Development Board has been established . . . if I say that I am Oriya, then I will not be acknowledged by the government and I will get nothing.[10] I look forward to an Oriya movement. But since no Oriya movement has started so far, I have to be an Adivasi.

The shift of allegiance from ACMS and ATTSA to the Adivasi movement, together with the fuzzy, overlapping, and flexible categories of tea tribes, Adivasis, Scheduled Tribes, tea plantation laborers, former tea plantation laborers, and so forth, creates a peculiar dynamic regarding the categories of the concerned agents of justice and subjects of justice. The trade union ACMS focuses on tea laborers as subjects of justice. It was established at a time when trade union movements and labor movements in India were booming and influential (Ahuja 2020). The Adivasi movement started as an ethnic or indigenous movement, which again resembles global trends (Della Porta and Diani 2006). Social movements with a focus on diverse identity categories beyond class started developing from the 1960s onward (Fraser and Honneth 2003). This move from "old" to "new" social movements has been characterized as a shift from class-based "materialist" claims, as in the trade union movement, to more "ideological" issues in identity-based movements, which challenge the dominance of the conflict between capital and labor, as well as the homogenous representation of people in classes (Buechler 1995). Indigenous movements with an emphasis on the diversification of identity categories beyond class have increased globally since the 1990s (Della Porta and Diani 2006) and have united across borders in their struggle to fight discrimination against Indigenous people as subjects of justice worldwide, as manifested in institutions such as the UN Working Group on Indigenous Populations, established in 1982 (Kikon 2017, 319).

All the interest groups working for tea plantation laborers (as subjects of justice) co-constitute a metagroup whose leaders as concerned agents of justice seek to represent the group's interests (objects of justice) in particular frames. Pierre Bourdieu (1989, 22–23) has described representation as the "power to make a new group . . . by speaking on its behalf as an authorized spokesperson." This "double representation"—creating a group by speaking on its behalf—shows that representation is always a *Vertreten* ("speaking for") and a *Darstellung* ("as in art or philosophy") (Spivak 1988, 275). Different kinds of representation or different ways of defining subjects of justice thereby create different mechanisms of inclusion and exclusion within justice regimes. Caste Hindus have occupied most leadership positions as concerned agents of justice in the trade union movement and "tea tribe" organizations. The Adivasi movement situationally adopted the use of "strategic essentialism" (Spivak 1988) to convince tea (and ex–tea) laborers to identify as Adivasi and thereby shift the subjects of justice, while granting only "true" Adivasis as truly concerned agents of justice access to leadership positions, and this enabled them to occupy important leadership positions for the first time in tea plantation history.[11]

Justice in Transition

In this chapter, I have analyzed different ideas about just working and living conditions for tea plantation laborers in Assam, which were prevalent among interest groups working on laborers' behalf during my fieldwork in India between 2014 and 2017. In the shifting political economy of tea production in Assam, the trade union ACMS promoted low cash wages with additional nonmonetary benefits to protect the tea plantation industry from a total collapse. Adivasi activists, who, since the 1990s, had fought for Adivasis to be acknowledged as Scheduled Tribes in Assam to make them eligible for affirmative action, have changed their object of justice to the implementation of the statutory minimum wage on tea plantations in Assam, criticizing the trade unionists as not really being concerned agents of justice for tea laborers.

Rather than providing a conclusive answer to the question of which idea of justice led to greater sociopolitical justice for tea laborers, I have drawn attention to the question of how visions of justice work at laborers' collective identities. I argue that, with the multiplication of objects of justice—from protecting the old-style plantation economy to promoting affirmative action to fighting for the implementation of statutory minimum wages for tea laborers in Assam—it was not only the better futures the interest groups envisaged for tea laborers that changed but also the categories of collective identification of subjects of justice and concerned agents of justice. Tea laborers as subjects of justice were designated either as "tea tribes," "Adivasis," or "labor rights' subjects" in different justice imaginaries. While being used as seemingly identical categories of identification, I contend that the categories were fuzzy and overlapping. This fuzziness allowed these categories to be used differently in different situations. Seemingly identical subjects of justice and concerned agents of justice turned out to be variable and flexible in different situations.

Adivasi activists advocated replacing the term *tea tribes* with *Adivasis*, which seemingly subsumed a large and inclusive group of people as its subjects of justice. However, in their hidden transcript, Adivasis differentiated between "real" Adivasis and "false" Adivasis to decide who was eligible for leadership positions or to be considered a legitimate concerned agent of justice in the Adivasi movement. Their situational adaptation of strategic essentialism resembled earlier strategies by the trade union movement that claimed to represent all "tea tribes" as subjects of justice but only allowed the caste Hindus among them to gain leadership positions or be concerned agents of justice in the trade union. The Adivasi movement and its members' visions multiplied objects of justice and leadership patterns in Assam. Justice imaginaries in transition changed not only objects of justice but also subjects of justice and concerned agents of justice that were declared to remain the same.

BUNGALOW DOCTRINES

Contrary to the famous principle by Bronislaw Malinowski (1922) that anthropologists must get off the veranda to conduct fieldwork, I had to get on the veranda to understand tea managers' conceptions of justice.

In the first part of this chapter, I discuss how tea planters (umbrella term for tea manager and tea plantation owner) and their relationship to tea laborers have been portrayed in the historical and contemporary literature on Indian tea plantations as being ambivalent between distance and proximity, while gestures of proximity have been interpreted as a means to exploit rather than be truly affectionate toward laborers. I will take a step back from these presuppositions and try to understand tea planters' justice imaginaries against the backdrop of their structural position in the tea industry more comprehensively. In the second section of the chapter, I show how planters themselves describe or reflect on their structural constraints, to argue in the third section that tea planters are situated between different regimes of justice that make sometimes contradictory claims on them. First, planters' ideas of justice, similar to laborers and trade unionists, are informed by the "old" welfare economy of tea production and the labor standards prescribed in laws such as the Plantations Labour Act or the Minimum Wages Act. Second, planters' notions of justice are informed by a principle of maximization of profits, which derives from their obligations to the tea companies for which they work. Third, tea planters' ideas of justice are also influenced by what one tea manager called "the bungalow doctrine"—a hierarchical principle of ruling that resembles structural casteism and classism. Rather than presuming "masks of benevolence" (Chatterjee 2001, 6) that are not truly affectionate but

FIGURE 13. Tea plantation manager's veranda. Photo by the author, Assam 2015.

only strategically instrumentalized to enforce coercive oppression, I suggest that managers' dilemma about how to act results from multiple regimes of justice that make different, at times contradictory, demands on them. Regarding the book's overall question of how justice works, this chapter illustrates that people are usually placed between multiple regimes of justice that may work either together or against one another and attribute different and sometimes contradictory obligations to them, which need to be weighed against one another.

Masks of Benevolence

In the literature on the colonial tea industry in Assam, different concepts have been evoked to characterize tea planters. The former British civil servant Percival Griffiths, who wrote one of the first comprehensive historical accounts of the Indian tea industry, characterized tea planters as "benevolent paternalists." Griffiths (1967, 376) asserted that the managerial tyranny at the initial establishment of the tea industry in the 1860s was replaced by "benevolent paternalism" a few decades later, when managers developed a sense of responsibility toward their laborers.[1] Griffiths had lived in India during the colonial time himself and had acted as a political adviser for the Indian Tea Association after his retirement from the Indian Civil Service. Therefore, he has been accused of having written from a perspective that is seen as friendly or biased toward tea planters by contemporary historians such as Rana Behal (2014, 9).

According to Behal (2010, 36), planters occupied a central position on plantations since they "were not merely employers of wage labor" but providers of houses, subsidized food rations, and space for leisure-time activities, and acted as adjudicates for conflicts on plantations. Accordingly, planters were involved in many aspects of laborers' daily life from a "position around which . . . the lives of the entire plantation community" revolved. Therefore, planters were also sometimes addressed as "planter *mai-baap*" (mother-father) (Chatterjee 2001, 6). However, Behal claims that this encompassing role of planters made laborers fully dependent on them and brought about the risk of managerial misuse of their position of power (Behal 2014, 103). Behal opposes Griffiths's image of tea planters as "benevolent paternalists," arguing that tea planters under the indentured labor system should more accurately be characterized as "coolie drivers" (105). The historian creates his concept of coolie drivers through an analogy to "slave drivers," based on his general argument that tea plantation labor in Assam under the indentured labor system was basically another form of slavery (see Behal 2010 and 2014). Behal sees the British managers on Assam's tea plantations as being not very different from former slave owners. In opposition to Griffiths, he argues that tea planters in Assam "were transformed into coolie drivers precisely during the period when the tea industry grew into a corporate business organization producing for the world market" in the late nineteenth century (Behal 2010, 32). He states that tea planters' attitude (individually and collectively) toward their laborers was shaped through their position in the tea industry. For instance, while half a million laborers worked on tea plantations in Assam by the end of the nineteenth century, only one thousand planters were present at the same time. According to Behal, this demographic gap created a secluded existence for planters and made them "keep their workforce docile, disciplined and intimidated" to uphold their authority (35). Next to arrest for any breach of contract, planters employed physical coercion (e.g., flogging), abusive language, and economic exploitation as measures to discipline laborers who did not act according to their expectations, and they justified their extralegal measures of controlling by saying that their companies had paid so much money to recruit laborers to the plantations in Assam— implicating a kind of entitlement to "own" laborers (37–39). Planters' role as coolie drivers was, according to Behal, backed up by the colonial state through the implementation of planter-friendly labor laws and different scales of justice for planters in cases of extralegal offenses (48). A reason for the solidarity between tea planters and colonial officials could have been their strong social bondage and "racial affinity," since both were part of a small community of upper-class Europeans in a distant land. The inhuman labor regime was, for Behal, not an exception but the rule, or the "characteristic of 'rational,' modern corporate capitalism" (50), in which planters needed to make profits by minimizing production costs for their companies to succeed in a competitive world market. Their most effective cost-minimizing strategy was to exploit labor and use coercive methods for intractable labor, effectively turning managers into coolie drivers (51).

In studies of present-day tea plantations in India, managers are described in similar ways. For example, Supurna Banerjee (2017, 3) describes managers as "patrons" or "benevolent father figures" to their laborers on the surface, but "behind this mask . . . lay a relation of coercion enforced through social distance, hierarchy of orders and a pyramidal social structure with the planter at the top." Similarly, the anthropologist Sarah Besky (2014, 64, emphasis in original) describes tea planters in her ethnography on Fair Trade tea plantations in Darjeeling as "paternal or avuncular figures" who "could be both oppressive *and* caring" from tea laborers' point of view. When, later in her book, Besky describes the manager of the first Fair Trade certified tea plantation in Darjeeling, she states that he "*styled himself* as a benevolent, enlightened caretaker and environmental steward," while he actually did not care for his workers (116, emphasis added).

The images of managers as patrons, paternalists, benevolent fathers, or avuncular figures emphasize the ambivalent character of managers in their relation to plantation laborers. On the one hand, managers are seen as caretakers for their laborers, which creates a hierarchical but nonetheless intimate relationship between managers and laborers. Managers are depicted as exploiting and abusing their laborers from a superior position in the plantation hierarchy. However, the benevolent aspect of managers, as was shown in the studies mentioned above (except for Griffiths), has been interpreted as a cloak to "morally justify the system of exploitation," as Behal framed it (103), or as a "mask" behind which "lay a relation of coercion," as Banerjee (2017, 3) stated. Thereby, benevolence is portrayed as a feature that is used to obscure a relationship that is *actually* coercive. Building on the existing literature on tea planters, I look at tea planters' position in the tea industry more closely in the next sections, based on the findings from my own fieldwork on the veranda.

Tea Planters' Position in the Tea Industry

According to historian Rana Behal (2014, 101), the first British tea planters came to Assam in the 1840s, either employed by joint-stock tea companies or as individual proprietors. By the late nineteenth century, the tea industry in Assam was almost exclusively under the control of British managing agencies based in Kolkata, which had their head offices in England. The British supremacy of Assam tea production and marketing endured until Indian independence (101–102). Many of the early British tea planters had lived in India before they became tea planters. They had worked in other occupations, as medical doctors, army officers, or colonial officers, among other things, before being attracted by the advantageous conditions offered for tea planters in Assam, including cheap and easy access to land and good terms for private capitalist enterprises, such as low taxation (105–106).

After the "indigenization" of the Indian tea industry that was initiated by the passing of the Foreign Exchange Regulation Act (FERA) in 1973, the last British planters left India. In the Assam tea industry, mainly higher-caste Bengalis, Assamese, or Marwaris subsequently took over the role of owners and managers. Owners are, not exclusively but often, based in Kolkata, where the tea companies' head offices are usually located. Nonetheless, owners travel to their tea plantations in Assam frequently to check if everything is in order. Managers, on the other hand, live on the tea plantations themselves.

"This Is Tea Garden Life!"

Mr. Puzaris is an executive plantation manager on a private tea estate in Upper Assam. He invited me to stay with him and his wife in their bungalow in January 2015 after I got acquainted with his daughter who was a master's student at Jawaharlal Nehru University, where I was a visiting fellow at that time. The plantation that Mr. Puzaris manages is of middle-scale, seven square miles in size with 600 permanent workers as well as 250 casual workers. Together with three other "sister" plantations in the same area, the plantation is co-owned by a Bengali and a Marwari businessman. The company's head office is based in Kolkata.

When I went to stay with Mr. Puzaris and his wife, they picked me up from the nearest bus stop in one of their three cars. We entered the plantation along the "company road"—usually the only tarred road on a plantation that guides visitors inevitably to the plantation factory, where the managers' offices are located. We drove past the factory and reached Mr. Puzaris's bungalow shortly after. The bungalow appeared huge and magnificent. It was surrounded by a large garden area with colorful flowers all over the place. Two of Mr. Puzaris's eighteen servants rushed toward me to help with my luggage. We entered the bungalow, passing a beautiful veranda with a canopy swing and an elegant seating area. When Mr. and Mrs. Puzaris showed me the guest room where I was going to stay, somebody served me a glass of water with a saffron flavor. They walked me through the bungalow's lavishly furnished rooms. While walking around, Mr. Puzaris declared, "This is tea garden life! It is not like normal life." Over dinner, he listed all the facilities that tea companies provide for managers and their families, such as a tennis club, golf club, and swimming pool. The companies provide the various amenities in regional "manager clubs." Tea managers from different companies, whose plantations are in the same region, meet regularly to hang out together in the "club" during their leisure time. Mr. Puzaris had been in the tea business for thirty-eight years when we met. He had studied up to LLB (Bachelor of Laws). He was from an Assamese (Ahom) family, and his father had worked for the Indian government as a tax officer. He explained that he had been attracted to the "tea garden life" when growing up in the area around Jorhat, where many tea gardens are located. This is why he had decided to become a tea plantation manager.

"Tea garden life" situates plantation managers at the interface between laborers and owners, who are often based outside of Assam. On the tea plantation site, managers occupy the highest position in the labor hierarchy, with one executive manager on top of his team of managers. Managers live in bungalows located at a distance from labor and staff quarters on the plantation. Like Mr. Puzaris, many managers were attracted to the "lordly" lifestyle that the tea companies provide for their managers, which resembles the lifestyle of the former colonial ruling classes. The benefits managers get include the bungalow compound, several cars, servants, and the leisure facilities in managers' clubs.

However, the quality of the facilities as well as the managers' salaries varies from company to company. Managers in state-owned plantations have the least attractive labor conditions and the lowest salaries in relation to others. The managers' salaries are fixed according to their work performance by the tea companies each year anew and are therefore usually kept confidential. Managers' salaries are therefore dependent on the profits generated by their companies at large. Managers were generally reluctant to disclose their salaries to me.

But one of my interlocutors estimated in 2015 that an executive manager in a government plantation in Assam earns about Rs. 50,000 per month and an assistant manager earns half of that. He estimated that executive managers in average private tea companies earn about Rs. 100,000 per month. The labor conditions for managers in leading tea companies such as McLeod Russel, Williamson Magor, Amalgamated Plantations, and Goodricke are better than in smaller and less prosperous private companies.[2]

Fed Up with Tea Garden Life

After Mr. Puzaris had initially described the "tea garden life" as marvelous to me, he later confided that he was actually "fed up with the tea garden life." Mr. Puzaris used to work and live on a better private tea estate but had had to take the manager's job on a comparatively less prosperous plantation after he had not performed well enough and generated sufficient profit for the company he previously worked for. Managers are constantly under pressure to produce an adequate quantity of good-quality tea. The owners hold them accountable for minimizing production costs while maximizing production outputs. If managers do not perform well, owners are able to downgrade their salary or dismiss them altogether, as was the case with Mr. Puzaris.

Managers fulfill multiple tasks on the plantation, which may be illustrated by my visit to another manager's office on Dolani Tea Estate. It was seven o'clock in the morning on a November day in 2016 when I was called to the manager's office to discuss something. The entry to Mr. Dimasa's office was closed only by a swinging door. Mr. Dimasa sat behind his desk facing the door wearing a camouflage-patterned bomber jacket. When I entered, he was talking to some bankers on the phone, arranging the delivery of money for his laborers' next weekly payment. The whole office was full of thick smoke since Mr. Dimasa chain-smoked. He indicated for me to sit on one of the chairs in front of his desk and rang a bell to order some chai for us. In the meantime, he finished his call, but various people kept entering and leaving his office with one or another issue at stake. A permanent laborer entered to suggest one of his relatives for a vacant driver's post. The welfare manager came to discuss some survey data with the manager, people came to get his signature for matters I did not understand, and finally the production manager came to announce that a government inspector had arrived. Mr. Dimasa excused himself; asked me to come back in the evening; rushed out of his office; jumped into his car together with an assistant manager, the driver, and his security guard; and raced off.

This hustle and bustle in Mr. Dimasa's office early in the morning is exemplary of managers' multiple tasks at work. These diverse tasks are a result of managers' position in the tea industry, which situates them between laborers and owners. On the one hand, managers are responsible for their laborers' welfare. They must ensure that laborers and staff are paid on time, organize the weekly subsidized food rations, hire new laborers, coordinate laborers, resolve conflicts, and take part in laborers' celebrations and ceremonies. On the other hand, they must manage tea production on the plantations and the prompt and most profitable disposal of their produced tea. They are responsible for ensuring that sufficient and high-quality tea leaves are grown and plucked in the fields despite any fluctuations in weather conditions. They must ensure that the fresh leaves are successfully processed into dried tea afterward in the factories. Managers must arrange transportation of undamaged tea to warehouses in Guwahati before they go to auction. They are accountable to the owners of the tea company for which they work, for producing tea that fulfills the quality standard to gain adequate profits from its sales. They furthermore deal with government inspectors or inspectors from certifying agencies who visit the plantation on a regular basis. The owners then negotiate tea sales with brokers who sell their tea in auctions and arrange additional private sales to direct buyers. One manager, commenting on the challenging nature of tea managers' multiple tasks, told me:

> I am sure I could do more for my people and my company, but because I am tied up in so many things . . . my work is very limited. My work is just to make the tea and make it arrive. I am only one small part, but I am the hardest part because I have to solve the problems of the laborers as well. I am doing all the donkey work. This is also what happened when they [the British companies] gave the tea gardens to the Indian counterparts and they went out. They wanted to keep the lucrative part of the business. They wanted to keep the tea selling in their own hands and wanted to give the garden management, which is tough, to whoever wanted to have the gardens.

Managers generally bemoaned the fact that managers' working conditions and amenities have deteriorated, making tea business a less appealing field of occupation than it was previously. One manager declared, "It was a great industry, but I feel that . . . it has deteriorated. I mean, it is not keeping up with the old days. People used to play horse polo and things. It was the most glorified industry in Assam. I mean, now we are still somebody. I mean, when you manage a tea estate, it is not that you are in the downtrodden part of society, but you are also not as respected as you used to be before." Mr. Puzaris once even said that he felt like a "first-class prisoner." He explained that he has all the luxury but cannot walk out of the plantation freely, and he only has the luxury as long as he is working as a manager, because when he retires, he will have to move off the plantation and will no longer be allowed to use the company's facilities. In this regard, managers face the same limitations as tea plantation laborers who receive benefits, such as housing, from the company only if they are an active part of its workforce. However, unlike the managers' prison, the workers' prison is not first-class.

Another major work challenge that managers mentioned to me is security threats. Since managers live secluded among hundreds or thousands of laborers, managers fear being attacked or killed by their workers. Smaller incidents of violence or threats of violence are more frequent, but incidents of killing, for example by setting a manager's bungalow on fire, happen comparatively seldom. The last such incident was reported in Assam in 2012 (Bhaumik 2012). But the possibility of murder causes serious tensions for managers, especially those who are managing a tea estate where a manager has previously been killed.

Further security threats to tea plantation managers have come from insurgency groups in Assam. The most difficult time in this regard was during the Assam agitation between 1979 and 1985. In 1979, some Assamese political and cultural organizations such as the All Assam Students Union (AASU) and the Assam Gana Sangram Parishad (AGSP) came together to demand the deportation of so-categorized illegal foreigners in Assam. Based on the observation that population growth in Assam appeared disproportionate in census data and electoral rolls, the joint groups of the so-called Assam movement demanded (partly with violent means) the disenfranchisement and expulsion of "foreigners" in Assam (Baruah 1986, 1184). Assam has a long history of partly controversial immigration of various people from other parts of India, such as Bengali Hindus from West Bengal, as well as Muslims from East Pakistan or later Bangladesh (Weiner 1983). The Assam agitation started with a general strike by the AASU on June 8, 1979, which initiated "unprecedented mass popular upsurge" (Baruah 1986, 1192). The Assam agitation ended with the Assam Accord, a Memorandum of Settlement between the government of India and leaders of the Assam movement (1203). Tea managers came under attack by militant groups related to the Assam movement, such as the United Liberation Front of Assam, for two reasons, according to the planters with whom I spoke. One reason they mentioned is that tea constitutes one of the biggest industries in Assam, and the militant groups were extorting money from tea managers to finance their movement. The other reason is that many tea managers are Marwaris from western India, who had migrated to Assam to work in the tea industry. Marwaris were seen by the nationalist activists from the Assam movement as "outsiders" who had come to "steal" the mineral resources and wealth from Assam and were therefore severely attacked. One tea plantation owner reflected on this time in the following way:

> They had kidnapped my uncle, they had kidnapped one of my managers, they shot two of my managers in the garden. Then we had a whole army and police force that we had to travel with. They had basically taken the industry hostage. We also suffered because when that hap-

pened, not only did we suffer that loss, we also had to sell one garden. . . .
We lost that garden because of extremism, which was almost shot every
day because the law-and-order situation was very bad.

A Bygone, Glorious Era?

All these challenges of a high workload with multiple responsibilities, an isolated and secluded life, and security threats have made a tea plantation manager's
job comparatively unattractive nowadays, according to the tea planters I interviewed. They said this was even more so since there are other, more lucrative and
attractive employment options nowadays for people from an educational and
social elite, which is the case for most tea planters. The days when tea companies
offered the most sought-after jobs in Assam were seen as a bygone era. A tea
plantation owner explained to me:

> The tea gardens are nowadays paying wages which are much lower than,
> say, telecommunication companies like Airtel and all—they pay much
> more. Earlier, the tea gardens were one of the most well-paid jobs. See,
> even me, today, I am thinking of looking for another job, because I am
> not earning enough. . . . It is not specifically a money-making venture.
> So, if you ask me today, if I had a small shop or hotel or something like
> that and I sold the tea garden, I would make more money. So, like that,
> most people are selling their assets and today, most tea gardens have
> changed ownership around three to four times since Independence.

According to this tea plantation owner, Mr. Chakraborty, the glorious era of
Assam tea has passed. I met Mr. Chakraborty in November 2015 through a friend
in Guwahati and asked him for an interview. He and his wife picked me up from
my residence for our interview, which was supposed to take place in his house.
His house was in the Kharguli hills—one of the most expensive residential areas
in Guwahati, which is based above the south bank of the Brahmaputra River. On
our drive, we passed a tea plantation. Mr. Chakraborty mentioned that this was
the last tea plantation his family owned. They used to own five tea plantations
in different parts of Assam but had sold all except this one plantation during
the last few years. They were considering selling this plantation as well, since its
acreage had turned into building land and therefore promised a high sales price.
When we approached Mr. Chakraborty's house at the top of the Kharguli hills,
at first sight it appeared to be a huge and impressive villa with several stories
and many intricate wings. The house must have been built during the colonial
time, since it displayed the typical colonial architecture style present in Assam,

with ornate wooden verandas and balconies, small protrusions, and large glass facades. When we got closer, however, I noticed that the house was in a bad condition. The house's facade and interior were totally decayed. I could easily see that no money had been spent on house maintenance for many years. The house somehow symbolized what Mr. Chakraborty told me about the tea industry during our interview. Its impressive architecture indicated the villa's former majestic splendor, while its current state of decay revealed that it belonged to a bygone era.

During our interview, Mr. Chakraborty confessed that indebtedness constituted a severe problem for him and his family, who used to own five average or lower-profit tea plantations. He stated,

> We have always struggled for money. We have never had excess money. We have always taken money on interest. This house has been in debt for twenty years. So, money is not easy for us. . . . In India, the interest rates are very high, we have to pay a minimum interest of 15 percent, which means that you have to make more than 15 percent profit to repay the bank. And right now, our profit margins are five percent to zero. Lots of tea gardens have diverted all these payments. So, when the good tea harvest years come, then all the money goes to paying back interest. And, suppose you do not even have a good crop, then again you go to the bank and take on interest, and after two or three years, you are in a trap. So, basically, you just have to work to pay your interest to the bank or brokers. So, from the planters' point of view, there is also a lot of problems. . . . We still have one garden, but we are thinking about selling it for a good price. . . . And you may think, why I would sell the garden? Because I think that the future is bleak!

Mr. Chakraborty's story offers some explanation as to why many tea plantations closed during the tea crisis that started in the 1990s. According to Mr. Chakraborty, in addition to this general crisis, Assam tea production was hit by the militant insurgencies that kept them busy with internal issues, while other tea-growing areas like Darjeeling found their way out of the crisis by moving to organic and Fair Trade tea production.

The planters' stories about a bygone glorious era of tea production resembles developments in the political economy of tea production in Assam. India's two largest tea producers in the twentieth century, Tata and Hindustan Unilever, withdrew from tea production in the 1990s by selling their plantations while continuing their engagement in tea branding and retail, which remained more profitable compared to tea production.[3] Against the background of this attempt to contextualize the structural position of tea plantation managers and owners in the tea industry in Assam, I analyze tea planters' justice imaginaries in the next section.

Embodied Casteism and Classism

The tea planters whom I interviewed imagined that just labor conditions on tea plantations would give tea laborers basic facilities including food, shelter, clothes, and health care. The list of amenities that planters said should be provided often resemble explicitly or implicitly the nonmonetary benefits prescribed in the Plantations Labour Act. The righteousness of providing laborers with basic facilities was emphasized by Mr. Puzaris, for example, when he juxtaposed British and Marwari planters. He asserted that, while British planters were "industrialists," Marwari planters were *only* "traders." Marwaris are traditional trading families from western Indian states like Rajasthan who came to Assam as tea planters in the twentieth century. Murleidhor Jalan, a Marwari who opened Dinjoye Tea Estate in 1923 in Dibrugarh, claims to be the first Indian tea planter. Assamese planters like Mr. Puzaris criticized Marwari planters for being "careless towards their laborers" because they were purely business minded and profit oriented. British planters, in contrast, had spent money on development and proper facilities for laborers, according to Mr. Puzaris.[4] The British were industrialists who followed a long-term and more humane vision of the tea plantation economy, while the Marwari "traders" were only concerned with quick profits.[5] These different evaluations of caretaking British planters versus careless and purely profit-oriented Marwari planters demonstrate that a pure orientation toward profit is seen as amoral, whereas taking basic care of laborers is considered a tea planter's obligation. In other words, the tea planter is seen as both the concerned and responsible agent of justice, required to provide his laborers (subjects of justice) with the basic labor rights (object of justice) due to them.

The tea plantation owner Mr. Chakraborty also admitted that "some people say that the [laborers'] conditions are okay, but I do not see that." To a certain extent, tea planters articulated being concerned about laborers' welfare and provision with basic facilities but felt unable to cope with its implementation. For example, Mr. Puzaris once stated:

> I tried so hard for many years. For example, I tried to raise the literacy level to total literacy, but I was only successful in raising it to about sixty percent. There are always two sides of one coin. We cannot manage to improve the situation by ourselves. The United Nations have to come and provide housing for the workers. The World Bank, the International Monetary Fund—they all have to come together and give them water and electricity. They have to come to promote the growth of the whole tea industry. The tea industry alone cannot bring about radical change with an annual profit of Rs. 1.5 crore. The increase of wages alone will not bring structural changes—social reform has to come. . . . I tried

so hard to improve the social system, education, their welfare. I built a playmobile for the workers' children. . . . It is not the companies who earn most. The brokers and the tea union are taking huge profits. If you want to bring radical change, then everybody has to join in—the government, NGOs and so forth. . . . Transformation is a distant dream. The WHO has to come for their health. Their hemoglobin is very low. The government has to provide them with their fundamental rights. The fundamental rights in India are guaranteed by the Constitution, Acts and the Supreme Court. They should also be provided.

According to this statement, Mr. Puzaris felt that fundamental rights are due to the plantation laborers. However, he thought that tea planters could not improve the situation by themselves. Because of his perceived inability to improve the situation, he addressed the Indian government, NGOs, and international organizations collectively as agents of justice who shared responsibility to give the laborers the basic facilities that were due to them. Thereby, Mr. Puzaris delegated responsibility for the tea plantation laborers' welfare away from tea planters. His argument was enhanced when he said he did not think that tea companies were the main profiteers in the industry but that tea brokers and tea unions were the ones who profited the most.

Mr. Chakraborty also commented on tea planters' structural constraints to change labor conditions fundamentally from the tea planters' position. He said,

Ultimately, we cannot do anything. Our job is how much we get paid, then we have to distribute the money and we keep a share for ourselves. And whether we are doing a fair job of that or not, that is all. I cannot come in with all the other factors like change the entire auction system or make sure that everybody in this zone is organic or make sure that Assam tea gets on that shelf. Those are not my jobs. My job is that whatever money I get from selling my tea, I have to distribute it. . . . It is a cutthroat world; everybody takes their share of the cake. And then we also adapt, and we also start to become harsher. We have to save our house and then those things do not start to matter to you—life of the laborers and all. There are so many hardships in your own life . . . so, even if you are thinking good and you've also got good intentions, after some time, you just can't do it. . . . Everybody has got a segment of jobs that we are contained in. That is why I feel that the welfare of those people should be left to themselves and they have to have their own groups if you really want to correct it within this system, because the system will not change all of a sudden. So, the way to change it is from them only. . . . We do whatever we can to make them a little happier, like organizing sports competitions or showing them movies. Somebody who marries, we loan them a little money. Somebody dies, sometimes we buy a coffin because they have no money. Those kinds of things we do, but by and large, we don't do much.

In this speech Mr. Chakraborty addressed the tea laborers themselves as being the agents of justice who were responsible for getting what was due to them, which seems as ironic as telling prisoners to free themselves. While Mr. Puzaris transfers responsibility for the workers' well-being from the tea planters to the government and international organizations, Mr. Chakraborty transfers the responsibility to the workers themselves.

Furthermore, unfair trade conditions for Assam tea were also held responsible for limiting tea planters' ability to bring about change for their laborers on plantations. For example, Mr. Chakraborty criticized the "outdated" and "primitive" tea auction system for selling Assam tea. Assam tea is sold either in Kolkata or Guwahati (where the auction center opened in 1970), and sometimes in Siliguri. According to an interview with the secretary of the Calcutta Tea Traders Association in 2016, the Tea Marketing Control Order of 1984 regulated that 75 percent of the produced tea had to be sold through auctions in India. After Bought Leaf Factories (BLF), to which the regulation had also applied, protested the regulation in the Madras High Court in April 2015, the regulation was amended in December 2015, so that only 50 percent of the tea produced by all manufacturers (BLF and estate factories) now must be sold through auctions. When I interviewed a member of the sales committee of the auction center in Guwahati in 2015, he explained to me that four actors are involved in tea auctions that need to be registered at the auction centers concerned: sellers, warehouses, brokers, and buyers. Sellers are either tea plantations or BLFs who deliver their produced tea in "lots" to warehouses based next to the auction houses.[6] Brokers, as the middle entity between sellers and buyers, take samples of the tea lots from the warehouses and send them to potential buyers. Buyers determine the price they are willing to pay for each tea lot by tea tasting. In the meantime, tea lots are cataloged and prepared for auction by brokers. During the weekly auction session, each lot is displayed for auction in the auction center or via e-auction. Based on their tea tasting, buyers decide beforehand which lots they want to bet on, with what stake. On the auction day itself, buyers only have ten seconds to bet on each lot. The buyer who bets the highest price gets the lot. Tea producers can give brokers a minimum price for each lot.

Mr. Chakraborty criticized the auction system for various reasons. First, he questioned the practice of determining tea sales prices by tea tasting.[7] Tea tasting is not conducted as a blind tasting; tea tasters are told the name of the tea plantation where the tea was produced. Mr. Chakraborty said that tea tasters were biased toward big tea producers and were prejudiced against smaller tea plantations. Since the tea tasters know the names of the producers and have expectations regarding the quality of tea, they would necessarily be biased. Furthermore, in his opinion, tea auctions were unfair because tea brokers released an advance payment of Rs. 70 to sellers as soon as their tea arrived at a warehouse. This meant that they were interested in selling the tea as swiftly as possible and sometimes undervalued tea just to get it sold quickly. Since tea producers had received an advance payment, they were trapped. The producers needed the advance payment to pay their tea laborers' wages on a weekly basis and did not have the money to pay them otherwise or wait until their tea was sold, which usually took around three weeks. Since they had spent the advanced money to cover their production costs by the time their tea was sold, they had a disadvantaged basis for negotiation and sometimes agreed to lower sales prices than they had intended. In addition, Mr. Chakraborty criticized the fact that tea sales prices as well as tea production costs and production outcomes varied tremendously due to the cyclic harvesting of tea and its dependence on external factors such as weather conditions, whereas tea plantation labor costs remained constant. He disapproved of tea being resold by retailers for ten times the price of what they, as producers, earned in their auction sales. If they got Rs. 600 instead of Rs. 200 per kilo of tea, Mr. Chakraborty claimed, then they would be able to pay their laborers Rs. 300 as daily wages.

However, tea planters were also hesitant about guaranteeing tea laborers' facilities beyond the most basic, because this could lead to a collapse of the tea industry—a contention that resembled the trade unionists' line of argumentation discussed in detail in chapter 4. Planters felt obliged to protect the industry by limiting laborers' remuneration. All the tea planters I met were against significantly higher cash wages for their laborers, in line with the official policy of the Consultative Committee of Plantation Associations (CCPA). An assistant manager explained to me that he opposed the introduction of a minimum wage because it would cause a tremendous raise in production costs, which would be bad for the tea industry:

> The Chief Minister announced the wage increase to Assam's minimum wage of Rs. 169, but we have not yet received any government order for its implementation. The CCPA will fight against its implementation. . . . It is the first time in history that we have seen such a huge jump in the wage increase and its impact is yet to be seen in future. Previously the

annual wage increase was never more than four or five rupees. . . . *This time law has given them too much!*

When managers were criticized for being against the introduction of the minimum wage, they sometimes presented a calculation sheet to prove that they were in fact paying the minimum wage if one considered all the nonmonetary benefits they paid. When, for instance, I asked a manager what he thought about the introduction of the minimum wage, he replied that they were already almost paying the requested wages if one calculated all the benefits and facilities on top of the daily monetary wages. This again resembles the trade unionists' statements in a remarkable way. The manager listed all the benefits and facilities in detail: food rations, free medical facilities, housing, blankets, footwear, aprons, education, drinking water, firewood, fourteen days' paid leave per year, and maternity and sick leave. However, managers included in their calculations facilities that were (at least partly) provided by the Indian government, not the tea companies. The Indian government, for example, provides primary education on plantations in addition to former company schools. Moreover, managers included facilities in their calculation sheets, such as housing or medical health care, that are explicitly excluded from the calculation of minimum wages, according to the Minimum Wages Act.[8]

This illustrates that managers were under pressure to act according to existing laws but were equally under pressure to gain enough economic profits to keep the tea industry going, which they tried to achieve by keeping wages low. Some planters claimed that, even if a tea planter supported the introduction of the minimum wage, they would not be able to implement the minimum wage on their plantation individually due to the structure of binding collective regional wage agreements for tea plantation laborers in Assam. But managers could push for the introduction of the minimum wage, for example, by advocating for it with the tea planters' union, which negotiates laborers' wages on behalf of tea planters. However, on the contrary, managers considered that the "law gives too much," as my interlocutor above stated. Another manager described what was meant by "law giving too much":

> They [the tea laborers] get maternity leave for three months—one month prenatal and two months postnatal. And the thing is, they get it unlimited even if they have six or seven children—and the consequence is that the workers have a child every year and misuse the regulations. . . . We were trying to limit the maternity leave regulation to two children but were not successful—it remains unlimited. This causes a colossal loss of money.

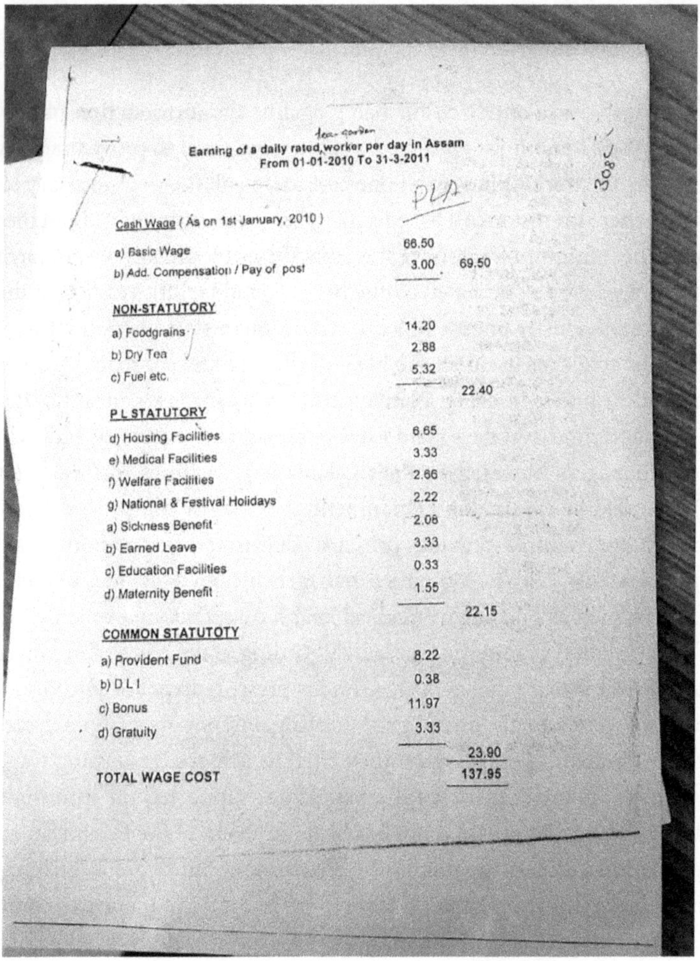

Earning of a daily rated worker per day in Assam
From 01-01-2010 To 31-3-2011

Cash Wage (As on 1st January, 2010)		
a) Basic Wage	66.50	
b) Add. Compensation / Pay of post	3.00	69.50
NON-STATUTORY		
a) Foodgrains	14.20	
b) Dry Tea	2.88	
c) Fuel etc.	5.32	
		22.40
P L STATUTORY		
d) Housing Facilities	6.65	
e) Medical Facilities	3.33	
f) Welfare Facilities	2.66	
g) National & Festival Holidays	2.22	
a) Sickness Benefit	2.08	
b) Earned Leave	3.33	
c) Education Facilities	0.33	
d) Maternity Benefit	1.55	
		22.15
COMMON STATUTOTY		
a) Provident Fund	8.22	
b) D L I	0.38	
c) Bonus	11.97	
d) Gratuity	3.33	
		23.90
TOTAL WAGE COST		137.95

FIGURE 14. Manager calculation sheets on tea plantation laborers' daily earnings. Photo by the author, Assam 2015.

This lack of limitation, according to the manager, caused a "colossal loss of money" because he believed laborers misused this legal loophole. He continued,

> We pay Rs. 25 per kilo of rice and the workers can buy it from us for 50 paisa. This is again unlimited: children get food rations no matter if the parents have five or ten children. This is a huge *injustice*. . . . We asked the government to stop their food rations because workers are provided with two food rations—one from the government and one from the companies. The workers take advantage of it and sell rice on the open market to get some extra money. The workers misuse government

schemes by selling subsidized food on the free market. The workers lack a civic sense and are abusing their status of being poor . . . The more you raise the workers' wages, the bigger is the production loss for the company—and the tea industry will eventually break down completely.

Although the laborers' behavior in this instance conformed with the law, the manager criticized it as an "exploitation of law" and a "huge injustice." Substantive legal labor regulations, which are granted by national law, thereby become bound to the deservedness of the laborers. Being a subject of justice is thereby bound to the defined moral righteousness of a person.

Mr. Chakraborty also accepted that there should be limits to laborers' welfare and upward social mobility in order to maintain the tea industry:

> We need to give some sort of tools to the laborers, so that they can work with less energy. We also need to give scholarships that send the intelligent kids from the community to Bangalore and all for their higher education. There are also positive stories—but they are very few. And, suppose that positive story was more, then nobody would work in the tea garden. If everybody comes out, that does not really help, who will work in the tea garden then? So, the job requirement is also that this community has to stay backward and has to stay like this.

Mr. Chakraborty's explicit statement that it was a tea planter's "job requirement" to keep tea plantation laborers backward is classist, since it advocates against low-class people's upward social mobility in general. Mr. Puzaris, who was extremely classist and casteist, went so far as to promote a "bungalow doctrine"—an embodied casteist and classist doctrine of hierarchical relations and forms of disciplining based on the premise that subordinate lower-class and lower-caste laborers, whom he dehumanized by calling them "two-legged animals," needed to be managed or ruled by a superior higher-class and higher-caste manager who lived in a distant and magnificent bungalow. He explained the bungalow doctrine to me in the following: "Workers have lousy habits of drinking and gambling. Their accountability is zero minus three. You have to rule the workers. The tea garden system and the aesthetics of ruling are gifts from the British. You have to have hierarchy in the tea garden to rule them successfully. . . . You can only rule and govern the workers when you live in a bungalow." Mr. Puzaris often expressed his admiration for the British and their "aesthetics of ruling," as well as his admiration for "great leaders" in general. He declared, "These people need strict ruling; they need punishments, otherwise they will misuse everything for their own advantage. They need a Hitler! There seems to be a new fundamental right: free wages, doing nothing. . . . They misuse the welfare laws!"

Justice in Conflict

In this chapter, I have outlined how tea planters have been characterized as being coercive despite wearing masks of benevolence to cover their coerciveness. I have described the structural position of higher-caste and higher-class tea managers placed between tea companies and lower-caste and lower-class laborers. A position that results in competing obligations in multiple regimes of justice that make different, sometimes contradictory claims on tea planters. I have argued that different regimes of justice have to be balanced by managers who, on the one hand, must maximize profit for their companies at a time when tea production is becoming less profitable and tea plantations are collapsing and being replaced by small growers who undermine labor standards and therefore produce cheaper tea. On the other hand, managers admitted that labor standards on plantations were not good enough and that laborers should be provided with basic facilities as prescribed by Indian labor laws. However, some (if not all) of the managers I interviewed demonstrated highly problematic classist and casteist attitudes toward the laborers, to justify their refusal to provide them with more than basic facilities.

Tea planters are typically seen as the primary responsible agents for ensuring fair labor and living conditions for tea workers. However, I argue that their ability to provide workers with what is owed to them varies depending on the prevailing regimes of justice. The tea planters I encountered during my fieldwork upheld hierarchical, casteist, and classist notions of justice, often dehumanizing tea laborers—for example, as "two-legged animals." I assert that planters possess the capacity to overcome structural casteism and classism, treat laborers with respect, which could foster greater confidence among workers and support their potential for upward social mobility. Regarding the material improvement of laborers' welfare, I contend that tea managers and tea plantation owners face more limited options for action. While tea planters could advocate for higher cash wages for tea laborers within the CCPA during the wage negotiations, they seem to be under significant pressure to generate sufficient profit to prevent the closure of their plantation. Once wage levels are set, individual managers lack the authority to pay workers more because the wage agreement not only sets a minimum but practically also an upper limit. Consequently, even if tea retailers such as the German Teekampagne wish to offer higher cash wages to the laborers from the plantation from which they purchase their tea, they are prohibited from doing so, as paying wages above the agreed limit in not allowed.

Iris Young has argued that structural responsibility for justice is turned into personal responsibility for justice when "the power of some actors is improperly inflated and that of many others is ignored" (Nussbaum 2011, xvi). While tea planters have responsibility for justice and a certain capability to act for a more just plantation economy, their responsibility seems to be inflated at times. Mr. Chakraborty once pondered that "there are a lot of issues and you cannot really pinpoint what is the main problem—whether it is the price of tea or whether it is the management who are doing wrong or whether it is their [the laborers'] own problem." Tea planters have the ability to change their casteist and classist attitudes toward laborers and advocate for higher cash wages, but their capacity to act is constrained by Indian labor laws, by fluctuations in global tea prices, and other factors. Therefore, if the entire responsibility for transforming the unfair system of tea production is placed solely on the tea planters, it is unlikely that the system will change in a way that benefits the laborers.

WORKINGS OF JUSTICE

Four different workings of justice—justice on scales, justice in context, justice in transition, and justice in conflict—have been analyzed in the present book to better understand what justice does "as an idea or a practice" (Brunnegger 2019, 4). These workings of justice have been deduced from observations made during my research on changing notions of justice in the transforming political economy of Assam's tea plantations. The conclusion offers some more general theoretical and practical considerations regarding the workings of justice. First, I explore how the four proposed workings of justice can be applied to analyze situations beyond Assam's tea plantations, assessing the broader theoretical implications of *justice at work*. Second, drawing from these theoretical insights, I suggest practical conclusions for Assam's tea plantations.

In chapter 1, I discussed the example of different justice scales within and beyond plantation "enclaves." Framing justice within plantation enclaves makes it easier to define objects of justice (Indian labor laws) and responsible agents of justice (tea planters). However, this narrower scale of justice runs the risk of improperly inflating the power of some actors while undermining that of others (Nussbaum 2011, xvi). Tea planters have a limited capacity to change the economic situation for Assam tea laborers at large. Upscaling justice beyond plantation enclaves makes a clear definition of objects of justice and responsible agents of justice more difficult but is more likely to address the multiplicity and complicity of regimes of justice at work. Upscaling justice thereby draws attention to structural classism and casteism beyond plantation enclaves when spacial mobility does not lead to upward social mobility for former tea laborers or their offspring. Upscaling justice also places Assam tea plantations into the global commodity chain of tea and global capitalism and demonstrates that tea planters are under pressure to keep labor costs low to produce tea in a profitable way, to prevent tea production on plantations from completely collapsing, leaving laborers and tea planters jobless. Abstracting from this concrete example, I argue that justice works differently on different scales. Justice regimes are more clearly defined and more likely to be implemented when they operate on a smaller scale than a broader one. However, justice regimes at lower scales risk overlooking more comprehensive justice issues. The way justice functions at different scales can be observed in other contexts. For example, the justice imaginary that people are due to fundamental rights works different on different scales. With the adoption of the Universal Declaration of Human Rights in 1948, fundamental rights were elevated from national constitutions to a universal level, declared as inalienable, and indivisible. However, this universalization makes it difficult to identify clear responsible agents of justice. At the national level, governments and the judiciary serve as the prime agents responsible for guaranteeing fundamental rights for their citizens. In contrast, at the global level, no single government or international human rights court holds direct accountability for ensuring the protection of human rights worldwide. Instead, so-called universal human rights can only be enforced indirectly—through national jurisdictions, regional human rights courts (e.g., European Court of Human Rights), national human rights institutions, additional protocols and complaint mechanisms, or the Universal Periodic Review. The challenge is that on a complex global scale, responsible agents of justice become much harder to identify compared to national jurisdictions. Moreover, the object of justice, such as fundamental human rights, are less clearly defined at the global level than within national legal frameworks. While the question of what exactly counts as a human right is not without controversy at the national level either, the definition of human rights at the international level is even more controversial and unclear. For instance, the status of third-generation human rights, such as the right to development, is widely debated. Questions arise about whether such rights should be recognized as human rights at all and, if so, how they can be effectively implemented. This illustrates how the object of justice in international human rights discourse is more ambiguous compared to more clearly listed fundamental rights found in national constitutions. However, while subjects of justice, responsible agents of justice, and objects of justice are more clearly defined at smaller scales, important justice-related issues may fade from view when limited to the national level. For instance, the right to development, a third-generation human right, addresses global inequalities that are not comprehensively covered by national constitutional rights. Similarly, noncitizens are only to a limited extent recognized as rights holders in national constitutions.

Ultimately, justice imaginaries work differently depending on scale—certain aspects of justice become more prominent, while others recede into the background, depending on the level at which justice is conceptualized and applied.

The second suggested working of justice—justice in context—is closely related to the first, but emphasizes slightly different aspects. I illustrated this by examining why tea laborers decide (not) to rebel, analyzing underlying notions of justice. When tea plantation laborers rebel, whether openly or covertly, they did so to maintain labor relations according to the old-style plantation economy at a time when it was undergoing transformations. Since the 1970s, the political economy of Assam tea has gradually shifted: from a scarcity of labor to a labor surplus, from being the world's largest tea exporter to becoming increasingly disarticulated from the global capitalist economy, from a plantation-dominated sector to the rise of smallholdings, from permanent labor contracts to a casual labor, and from welfare labor laws to a new labor law regime that dismantles those laws characterized by extensive social welfare measures. I have argued that, within this transformed political economy, laborers' efforts to preserve the old-style plantation economy are shifting from a structure-preserving mode to a structure-undermining one. Working modes of justice vary depending on the economic and social structures in which they are situated. When the tea plantation economy is largely regulated by the Plantations Labour Act, adherence to its labor principles maintains existing plantation structures. However, as tea production has evolved toward even more precarious working conditions, such as on smallholdings, labor ideals based on the Plantations Labour Act may no longer work to maintain the given structures because the structures do no longer exist. Placed into a new political economy of tea production, holding onto on old-style plantation economy rather undermines given new structures. Justice imaginaries can work differently depending on the spatiotemporal context. Similarly, for example, advocating for Islamic justice imaginaries in a Muslim-majority country can be structure-preserving, while in a Catholic-majority country, it may be subversive.

Third, I have demonstrated how changing notions of justice impact categories of collective identification, by discussing activist campaigns for tea plantation laborers. Activists officially claim to be changing the objects of justice (from maintaining the tea plantation economy to guaranteeing affirmative action to implementing minimum wages) in order to bring justice closer to tea plantation laborers. Activists assert that the subjects of justice basically remain the same despite their terminological shift from "tea tribes" to Adivasis to labor rights subjects. Moreover, activists suggests that the subjects of justice and the concerned agents of justice who are designated by the same terminology, include the same kind of people. However, I have illustrated the strategic benefit of including and excluding different people in seemingly identical categories of collective identification in different situations. While "tea-tribe" activists claim to promote the welfare of all "tea tribes," they only allow mainly male caste Hindus to have higher leadership positions. While Adivasi activists claim to speak on behalf of all Adivasis, they only allow "real" Adivasis into leadership positions. Therefore, "tea tribes" as subjects of justice are not identical to "tea-tribes" as concerned agents of justice due to flexible situational adaptations of categories of collective identification when seemingly only the objects of justice, not the subjects of justice and concerned agents of justice change. How justice imaginaries are related to categories of collective identification can be discussed beyond the tea plantations in Assam—for example, with reference to the discussions about the integration of more groups under the Scheduled Tribes category in Assam. As mentioned in chapter 4, there is a debate in Assam as to whether more groups in Assam should be recognized as Scheduled Tribes. Scheduled Tribe is an administrative category in the Indian constitution intended to strengthen minority rights of historically discriminated groups. Since Scheduled Tribes in other Indian states are often Adivasis, Scheduled Tribes are sometimes equated with Indigenous people. In Central India, historical marginalization and indigeneity often coincide. In Assam, however, Indigenous people like Thai Ahom are former rulers in Assam, which means that there is a discrepancy between indigenousness and historical marginality. If Thai Ahom were recognized as Scheduled Tribes in Assam, terminologically the category of Scheduled Tribes would remain the same. However, since the constitution of the Scheduled Tribes as subjects of justice would de facto change by including historically privileged groups, the imaginary of justice (as what is due to whom) would change significantly, even though it is conceptually negotiated in the same terms. The third working of justice illustrates that categories of collective identification within justice imaginaries are transforming, situationally and flexible adaptable. Changes in the constitution of who is subsumed under a category of collective identification such as subjects of justice may affect objects of justice and vice versa.

Fourth, by looking at the different "bungalow doctrines" at work among tea planters, I have demonstrated that people are placed between multiple regimes of justice that make different, and at times conflicting, claims on the person. When people balance different regimes of justice, they work together or against one another and influence the extent to which regimes of justice are implemented in practice. Instead of seeing tea planters' affection toward laborers as a "mask of benevolence" in order to force coercive measures onto tea laborers, I have suggested that different regimes of justice pull on tea managers and contradictory demands move tea planters to make compromises within the multiple regimes of justice. For instance, while tea planters agree with basic facilities for tea laborers as prescribed by the PLA, they do not really support providing facilities beyond a basic level because they are afraid that more facilities would affect the profitability of tea production and eventually jeopardize the continued existence of tea plantations, which is the worst-case scenario not only for them but also for tea laborers because there are neither manager bungalows nor labor lines outside the plantation economy. However, whereas the provision of welfare justice for laborers is limited by the managers' obligations toward the tea companies to make profits, I have argued that managers had a bigger scope of action with regard to changing their classist and casteist attitudes toward the laborers, which support argumentatively the limitation of welfare facilities provided for laborers by planters. People are always positioned between different justice imaginaries that either work together or conflict with one another. I argue that the perspective of positioning (concerned and responsible) agents of justice between conflicting justice imaginaries can help to prevent interpreting capitalist tea planters' imaginaries of justice as one-dimensionally exploitative, interpreting every human emotion of affection as a "mask" to disguise one's own exploitative agenda. A justice in conflict perspective does not suggest advocating or appeasing the capitalist exploitation of tea planters. The perspective rather wants to admit to capitalists that they are multidimensional, as are all actors. The fourth working of justice dimension as justice in conflict thus represents an analytical category for examining multidimensionality, which is granted not only to those who already seem sympathetic anyway.

Practical Conclusions

From these theoretical conclusions on how justice works, I draw some more practical conclusions on "plantation futures" (McKittrick 2013). First, I do not consider the replacement of colonially inherited large-scale tea plantations in Assam with smallholdings as a solution that is beneficial for tea plantation laborers unless (former) tea plantation laborers are enabled to become small growers themselves. I found that smallholders in Assam were more likely to be local Assamese people than (former) tea plantation laborers. While it may be seen as a positive development for local Assamese people to become small growers, it is the former ruling classes that are profiting from that development rather than historically marginalized tea plantation laborers and their offspring. Second, I suggest that minimum wages in the tea industry in Assam should be only minimal standards and not de facto maximal limitations. This would allow foreign tea purchasers to pay higher cash wages to the laborers from whose plantations they purchase their tea, instead of supporting laborers indirectly through welfare measures that are supposed to be paid by the Indian state anyway. Third, consumers should be willing to pay more money for a cup of tea if ways are created to channel the added value directly to the tea plantation laborers—for example, through trade agreements that enable higher cash wages to be paid beyond minimum wage agreements.

Creating New Best Among Worse Alternatives

Justice at work is an attempt to explain unlikely alliances between tea plantation workers, trade unionists, and tea planters. This allows to see the multidimensionality of all actors "at work" on Assam tea plantations. It is an attempt to illustrate that since justice works different on different scales, a critique limited to plantation enclaves that addresses tea plantation managers as responsible agents of justice improperly inflates the managers' odds to act in bringing justice to tea laborers and does not pay sufficient attention to the fact that tea laborers are subject to classist and casteist discrimination outside plantation enclaves. Therefore, spacial mobility does often not lead to social upward mobility. To call for repealing capitalist plantations (which is happening anyway) may create a worse scenario for tea workers. Tea plantations workers' will to maintain the "old-style" plantation economy together with trade unionists and tea planters works structure-undermining and not structure-maintaining at a time of legal and economic transformations of tea production on plantations in India. Therefore, instead of suggesting to overcome exploitative plantation economies and leave plantation workers confronted with worse alternatives such as working for small growers or being exposed to severe casteism and economic precarity as farmers in rural areas, I hope for more encompassing structural transformations that create a world in which maintaining "old-style" plantation economies is not seen as the best among worse alternatives for tea plantation laborers.

Notes

INTRODUCTION

1. All names of persons and places in this book are pseudonyms.

2. The labor quarters, or the areas of the plantation where the plantation laborers' residential houses are located, are called "labor lines."

3. Permanent tea plantation laborers were usually entitled to decide whom to "inherit," that means to pass on their permanent position after their retirement.

4. Daily wages amounted to Rs. 94 in 2014. In 2015, the ACMS had agreed to a wage increase to Rs. 115, which was below the statutory minimum wage of Rs. 169 at that time.

5. *Tea planter* is an umbrella term for tea manager and tea plantation owner. While sometimes one person holds the office of a plantation manager and owner at the same time, plantation managers more often live on the plantation to supervise the production of tea and tea owners have their offices elsewhere in bigger cities such as Guwahati or Kolkata.

6. By "differently positioned actors," I do not suggest an essentialized understanding of different actors. I want to emphasize that actors' structural positionalities in the context of the tea plantations are related to their positions (here with regard to justice imaginaries). It has been widely discussed whether positions are determined or conditioned by positionality or whether positions can develop to a certain extent independently of positionality and whether a certain positionality can produce epistemologically privileged insights or more objective knowledge. With regard to the first question, some approaches take the view that positions result of positionality, which leads to a (radically) structurally deterministic or (moderately) structurally conditioned reproduction of social (unequal) relations (Bourdieu 1977). Other approaches have postulated that marginalized people have a privileged epistemological positionality (e.g., Du Bois 1903; Haraway 1988; Harding 1992).

7. Gorkha are Nepalis living in India who claim the establishment of a separate Indian state ("Gorkhaland") carved out of West Bengal. See Wenner 2013.

8. In the tripartite moral economy, laborers distinguish principles of *industri* and *bisnis*. The tripartite moral economy manifests itself for laborers in the *industri* model of plantation economy. In the *industri* version of plantation economy, planters are entitled to profits, but they also reinvest capital into the landscape and labor force by providing facilities rather than monetary compensation (Besky 2014, 63). *Bisnis*-men, on the other hand, are only interested in extracting from land and labor in the *bisnis* model of plantation economy. Accordingly, laborers evaluate plantations guided by a principle of *industri* as moral and plantations guided by a principle of *bisnis* as amoral. A transition seen by planters, in contrast, as "a revitalization of the tea industry" (62).

9. Sen (2017, 11–12) defines "everyday sustainability" as "practices and processes through which women actively learn about emerging market-based sustainability and justice regimes and evaluate their effectiveness in addressing their everyday community-level struggles over resources, representation, and entrepreneurship."

10. Sen illustrates the meaning of *swaccha vyāpār* as one justice imaginary of smallholder women tea farmers in chapter 6 of her book. Smallholder women tea farmers had formed a cooperative in 1997 that was registered and certified as Fair Trade in 2007. Sen

observed a Fair Trade certifier visiting the cooperative to see whether conditions for certification were still met. The cooperative's governing board—the highest decision-making body—consisted exclusively of men. Women farmers were represented in the cooperative's Women's Wing below the governing board. The Women's Wing had asked the governing board to give them a share of the Fair Trade premium money, which the governing board had refused. During his visit, the Fair Trade certifier criticized the cooperative's gender inequality and suggested disbanding the Women's Wing and representing women on the governing board. After the women rejected this, the cooperative's Fair Trade certification was put on probationary status. The women explained to Sen that they had rejected the certifier's suggestion because a few women on the governing board would not have been able to bring about change because they would have been outvoted by men. Through their rejection, they successfully protested the governing board's refusal to share the Fair Trade premium money with them. The governing board afterward agreed to share the premium with the Women's Wing.

11. Jegathesan's solidarity with the workers seems to be based on their shared Tamil womanhood and not compromised by "the fact that the Sri Lankan Tamil communities to which I am linked by blood and heritage were and remain directly implicated in ongoing forms of caste discrimination against Hill Country Tamils communities today" (Jegathesan 2019, 31–32).

12. In the introduction to our Special Issue "Justice in the Anthropocene," we build on debates in the new anthropology of justice (e.g., Brunnegger 2019; Clarke and Goodale 2009; Johnson and Karekwaivanane 2018) to propose an analytical definition of justice. Approaches in the new anthropology of justice aim to develop a concept of justice that is both ethnographically grounded and theoretically substantiated. For instance, Sandra Brunnegger (2019, 15) coined the term *everyday justice* to frame justice as multifarious, spatiotemporally contingent, indeterminate, and dynamic, arguing thereby "not to privilege any particular epistemological or ontological tradition" (4). While we consider it important to complement established theories in political philosophy with ethnographically substantiated theories of justice, we content that characterizing justice as multifarious is not value-free and has serious theoretical limitations. Without a more specific analytical definition of justice, researchers are either arbitrarily constrained to look at settings where people happen to use the word *justice* themselves (whether in English or in local translation) or to follow their own implicit notions of justice when trying to locate justice empirically. In other words, abstaining from explicitly defining justice does not mean that researchers do not implicitly apply their own definitions. Therefore, we propose a distinctive analytical definition of justice for studying the empirical plurality of justice.

13. The activists' agenda to bring justice close to marginalized communities in India must be understood in the context of a shift toward people-centered development after the Sustainable Development Goals included the provision of "access to justice for all" in Goal 16.

14. This is similar to the suggestion by David Leslie Miller (2021) that "the constant and perpetual will to render to each his due" would express an essential feature of an analytical definition of justice that is "present whenever justice is invoked" while acknowledging that justice takes "different forms . . . in various practical contexts."

15. This is in reference to E. P. Thompson's reading of moral economy (Thompson 1971). There are many different understandings of moral economy. For instance, Didier Fassin (2009, 14) emphasized the "moral" instead of the "economy" in understanding moral economy as "the production, distribution, circulation, and use of moral sentiments, emotions and values, and norms and obligations in social space."

16. The difference I state here between desire and justice is somehow similar to how Julia Eckert (2023, 448–449) has differentiated moral and legal responsibility. While

moral responsibility is of voluntary nature, legal responsibility implies binding obligations and deeds.

17. Although no reliable and current statistics are available on the present-day social composition of the labor force on Assam's plantations, there are some estimations that resemble the historical census data and my own microscale estimations drawn from field-work. Walter Fernandes (2003), for instance, estimates that Adivasis constitute roughly 50–60 percent of the plantation labor force. Apart from Adivasis, Dalits and caste Hindus constitute the remaining labor force. The ethnic division roughly resembles religious belonging. While Adivasis are more likely to be Christians, Dalits and caste Hindus are more likely to be Hindus. The separation between the different ethnic, caste, or religious groups on plantations is upheld through endogamous marriage practices. Endogamy is practiced not only among religious groups but also among religious denominations. Catholics, for example, are not allowed to marry Baptists. These rules are broken on a regular basis, but the fact that couples from different denominational backgrounds needed to publicly apologize for the transgression demonstrates that endogamy is at least upheld ideologically. The multiple categories of collective identification of Assam tea workers are discussed at length below and in chapter 4.

18. The indentured labor system and the migration of indentured laborers are elaborated in chapter 1.

19. According to his great-granddaughter, the first Indian planter in Assam was Murleidhor Jalan, who started the Dinjoye Tea Estate in 1923 in Dibrugarh (interview with Avantika Jalan on April 22, 2021).

20. Expressed in general terms, Assamese denotes the descendants of former ruling classes in Assam during the Ahom kingdom, Bengalis come from the neighboring Indian state of West Bengal, and Marvaris are traditional traders from western India.

21. The PLA was amended in 1953, 1960, 1961, 1981, 1986, and 2010. For Assam, the regulations of the PLA were further elaborated in the Assam Plantations Labour Rules of 1956.

22. Bilateral agreements between ACMS and CCPA in the twentieth century were fixed in 1966, 1969, 1970, 1973, 1974, 1976, 1980, 1983, 1993, 1996, and 2000 (Mishra et al. 2012, 105). Initially, wages in Assam were differentiated between six different zones, in which the wages differed between one and two rupees (Xaxa 1996, 24). Today, wages in Assam only differ between the Assam Valley and Cachar in South Assam.

23. This process was supported by Structural Adjustment Programs in Kenya, for example, by the World Bank and International Monetary Fund that forced Kenya to prioritize on tea and coffee production at the expense of food security from the mid-1980s onward. Eventually, Kenya became the largest tea exporter worldwide. Kenya almost exclusively produces tea for export (Raman 2010, 152).

24. In his rich ethnography, Jayaseelan Raj (2022) describes in detail how Dalit Tamil tea plantation workers in Kerala navigated the plantation crisis and the subsequent transformations on the plantations.

25. There are no reliable, consistent, and current statistical numbers available on Assam's tea plantations. Statistical numbers given are always to be understood as rough estimations since they vary depending on the source. Moreover, methodological reflections about how these numbers have been generated are largely absent. Sharma and Das (2009, 124) estimated that there were 850 tea plantations in Assam in 2009 while Dikshit and Dikshit (2014) estimate more than 900 large-scale commercial estates in Assam. A newspaper article states that there were 792 registered tea plantations in Assam (Bolton 2018). The estimation is particularly difficult because the statistical data provided by the Tea Board of India has included small growers in the listed number of tea plantations in India since 1998 without differentiating large estates and small growers. Estimates here

are taken from Government of Assam Tea Tribes Directorate for Welfare, List of Tea Gardens at Assam: https://ttwd.assam.gov.in/frontimpotentdata/list-of-tea-garden-at-assam (accessed September 16, 2024); and Government of Assam Directorate of Economics and Statistics, Economic Survey of Assam 2017–18: https://des.assam.gov.in/information-ser vices/economic-survey-assam (accessed May 23, 2021).

26. I thank Ravi Ahuja for helping me to articulate this thought more clearly.

27. Jaipal Singh is important for Adivasi politics in postcolonial India because he fought for his convictions that Adivasis are India's "original inhabitants," are marginalized by non-Adivasis in India, and should be compensated for their historical discrimination (R. Guha 2008, 115). He founded the Adivasi Mahasabha in 1938, which later became the Jharkhand Party, and fought for the establishment of Jharkhand as a separate Adivasi state in India (267).

28. I am thankful to the second anonymous reviewer for encouraging me to draw more general conclusions about *justice at work*.

1. SCALES OF JUSTICE WITHIN AND BEYOND PLANTATION "ENCLAVES"

1. The term *jāt(i)* literally means "birth." It is used to describe lineages or endogamous groups in India located in hierarchical relation to one another and to indicate spiritual (im)purity (Michaels 2012, 189–191). In colloquial language, the term *jāti* is often used interchangeably with the term *caste*. In my fieldwork in the plantation context, both terms were used to denote ethnic communities of different scopes, including Adivasis.

2. For a critical discussion of the term *coolie*, see Jegathesan 2019, 12–15. See also Breman 1989, Breman and Daniel 1992, and Varma 2016.

3. I follow Bourdieu's (1998) understanding of precarity as a labor condition rather than Butler's (2006) reading of precarity as an ontological condition. For an excellent discussion of the different meanings and politics of the term *precarity*, see Millar 2017.

4. The term *kaṣṭ* is generally used in India to express a feeling of suffering or hardship. It is not particular to tea plantation labor.

5. The retirement scheme includes gratuity and a provident fund (combination of workers and companies' contribution).

6. Haraway suggested replacing the term *Anthropocene* with the term *Plantationocene* rather spontaneously in a conversation about the Anthropocene among anthropologists at the University of Aarhus in October 2014, which was published two years later in *Ethnos* (Haraway et al. 2016). She later described the Plantationocene as a "situated historical metabolism with the planet in conditions that nurture extraction and extermination" (Paulson 2019).

7. I suggest the term *structural casteism* in analogy to structural racism. Structural racism draws attention to structural discrimination. It is therefore not (only) about individual and conscious racist actions and attitudes but (primarily) about largely unconscious structural privileges and disadvantages that exist due to racism. This includes seemingly banal everyday occurrences such as the universal term *skin color*, which assumes a certain skin color as the norm without reflecting this. Structural racism involves an appeal to provincialize such supposedly universal norms (Harrison 1991). Furthermore, structural racism implies critical reflection by those disadvantaged by structural racism that certain seemingly personal disadvantages are structurally conditioned. For example, a rejection for a job may be due not to personal failure but rather to (sometimes unconscious) racist discrimination. Likewise, structural racism requires those who are advantaged by structural racism to be aware of their own advantage at the expense of the structural discrimination of others (Wekker 2016; DiAngelo 2018). By analogy, I use the term *structural casteism* to refer to structural advantages and disadvantages based on caste, which are often subconsciously overlooked, as well as the generalization of particular (Brahmanical) perspectives.

8. In his monography *Plantation Crisis* (esp. ch. 4), Jayaseelan Raj (2022, 80) emphasizes the "hidden injuries of caste" for Tamil Dalit tea workers inside and outside tea plantations in Kerala.

2. LIVING FROM THE TEA LEAVES

1. For instance, Tobias Kelly (2008, 358) illustrated the hard work of maintaining everyday life when describing how Palestinians in the West Bank went to great lengths to circumvent Israeli checkpoints during the second Intifada.

2. Hundi seems to be similar to other kinds of informal economic networks and collectives that others have described elsewhere in different terms, such as *ghumāuri* (see Sen 2017).

3. Tea companies in Assam give 1.5 kilos of rice and an equal amount of whole wheat flour to each adult permanent worker per week and half that amount of rice and flour for each child. The government additionally distributes monthly food rations for families who are categorized as "Below Poverty Line" (BPL)—most (but not all) tea plantation workers are categorized as BPL. For a general introduction to government measures for poverty reduction in India, see Bertram 2012.

4. Data from ILOSTAT by the International Labour Organization: https://ilostat.ilo .org/data/. Accessed September 18, 2024.

5. As mentioned above, reliable statistical data is hardly available on Assam tea plantations. Mishra et al. (2012) estimated that around 50 percent of the laborers in Assam are male and 45 percent female. Five percent of tea laborers are listed as adolescent without a gender specification (96). Children (younger than fourteen years old) were also officially employed on plantations in Assam until 2010, and child labor was much higher in Assam than in other tea-growing regions in India (102). The employment of children was prohibited by the last amendment to the Plantations Labour Act in 2010, following the preceding abolition of child labor in India by the Child Labour (Prohibition and Regulation) Act of 1986. Statistics from other tea-growing regions in India suggest that more than half of the tea laborers are female (see, e.g., Banerjee 2021, 62).

3. WHY TEA PLANTATION LABORERS DO (NOT) REBEL

1. There is a long debate in the anthropology of resistance about whether actions that are not framed as resistance by the actors themselves can justifiably be labeled as such (see, e.g., Wright 2023). I follow Scott's evaluation that they can analytically be called everyday forms of protest without denying that the acts can be interpreted differently from other points of view.

2. Reemtsma (1999) differentiates between legal feelings ("Rechtsgefühle") and feelings of justice ("Gerechtigkeitsgefühle"). "Rechtsgefühle" are aimed at restoring a legal order after the sense of justice has been shaken by punishing the perpetrator. The transformation of the "Gerechtigkeitsgefühl" into a "Rechtsgefühl" goes hand in hand with a shift in perspective, in which victims no longer see themselves exclusively as injured individuals but as participants in a legal community.

4. JUSTICE AND CATEGORIES OF COLLECTIVE IDENTIFICATION

1. For a detailed general discussion of the categories of collective identification such as Adivasi, Scheduled Tribes, tea tribes, see introduction.

2. In South Assam, the Cachar Chah Sramik Union is the acting trade union. It is also affiliated with INTUC. Since the Bharatiya Janata Party (BJP) won the Assam Legislative Assembly elections in 2016 for the first time and in 2021 again, the BJP-related Bhartiya Chah Mazdoor Sangha has gained influence.

3. Other studies on the political economy of capital-labor relations in India have analyzed trade union strategies in collective bargaining and demonstrated how trade unions in fact undermine labor rights despite articulating their dedication to the laborers' interests (see, e.g., Chakraborty et al. 2019).

4. The ACMS has started to support minimum wages since then. Unfortunately, I was unable to conduct follow-up interviews with trade unionists after their change of direction.

5. Affirmative action is an attempt "to compensate for past discrimination and minimize existing inequalities that persist on the basis of group identity . . . to create the conditions for disadvantaged groups to compete equally" (Shah and Shneiderman 2013, 3–4).

6. For an excellent discussion of indigeneity, see Zenker 2011.

7. The names of the international NGOs are intentionally not mentioned to keep them anonymous. The founders and leaders of the NGOs were either foreigners or higher-caste Hindus.

8. Tea plantation laborers in the Assam Valley have earned Rs. 250 since 2023. Laborers in the Barak Valley have earned Rs. 228 since 2023.

9. In 2011, Oriya people and the Oriya language were renamed "Odia," and the federal state of Orissa was renamed "Odisha."

10. The Adivasi Welfare and Development Council was finally established in 2022 following the Adivasi Accord signed on September 15, 2022.

11. Spivak (1988, 205) defines strategic essentialism as "a strategic use of positivist essentialism in a scrupulously visible political interest," while Zenker (2016, 295) refines it as "the stance of theoretically rejecting homogenising, reductive and atemporal categories, while politically endorsing them for situated struggles."

5. BUNGALOW DOCTRINES

1. The period from 1860 to 1865 was called "tea mania" because of the massive expansion of tea plantations in Assam during these years. It was characterized by the tea industry's chaotic organization, due to its uncoordinated growth (Behal 2010, 34).

2. The English names of tea companies are misleading. Many tea companies kept their English names after the "indigenization" of the tea industry in India in the 1970s. However, according to an interview with the general secretary of the Calcutta Tea Traders Association in 2016, the majority of the companies' shareholders are Indian citizens today, with the exception of Goodricke.

3. Tata has only indirectly divested from tea production, having established a new tea-producing company called Amalgamated Plantations Private Ltd. (APPL) in 2007. APPL introduced a new model of shared ownership among tea employees (the transition from Tata to APPL included the sale of up to 30 percent of the shares to employees including management, staff, and workers) as well as commodity diversification beyond tea. For further information and a critique of APPL, see Columbia Law School 2014.

4. The Jalan family has a different self-perception. The great-granddaughter Avantika Jalan sees a "unique relationship" between their family, who stayed on their plantations for generations, and the "labor community."

5. See also Sarah Besky's chapter on the tripartite moral economy of tea plantation laborers in Darjeeling (Besky 2014, chap. 2), which makes a similar distinction between "industri" and "bisnis."

6. A "lot" consists of at least twenty bags of tea of the same quality and grade.

7. Sarah Besky (2020) published an insightful study of tea tasting.

8. For more details on the Minimum Wages Act, see the introduction in this book.

References

Ahuja, Ravi. 2020. "'Produce or Perish': The Crisis of the Late 1940s and the Place of Labour in Postcolonial India." *Modern Asian Studies* 54 (5): 1041–1112. doi:10 .1017/S0026749X17001007.

AK, Aditya. 2015. "How a Group of Lawyers and Activists Are Bringing Assam's Tea Labourers Closer to Justice." *Bar and Bench*, November 16. Accessed November 17, 2015. http://barandbench.com/how-a-group-of-lawyers-and-activists-are -bringing-assams-tea-labourers-closer-to-justice/.

Ali, Subhashini. 2011. "Indians on Strike: Caste and Class in the Indian Trade Union Movement." *New Labor Forum* 20 (2): 32–39. doi:10.4179/NLF.202.0000006.

Ananthanarayanan, Sriram. 2010. "Scheduled Tribe Status for Adivasis in Assam." *Journal of South Asian Studies* 33 (2): 290–303. doi:10.1080/00856401.2010.494823.

Bair, Jennifer, and Marion Werner. 2011. "Commodity Chains and the Uneven Geographies of Global Capitalism: A Disarticulations Perspective." *Environment and Planning A* 43 (5): 988–997. doi:10.1068/a43505.

Banerjee, Supurna. 2017. *Activism and Agency in India: Nurturing Resistance in the Tea Plantations*. London: Routledge.

Banerjee, Supurna. 2021. "'Who Leaves Home If There Is a Choice?' Migration Decisions of Women Workers on Tea Plantations in India." *Transfers* 11 (2): 53–75. doi:10.3167/TRANS.2021.110205.

Banerji, Sabita, and Robin Willoughby. 2019. "Addressing the Human Cost of Assam Tea: An Agenda for Change to Respect, Protect, and Fulfil Human Rights on Assam Tea Plantations." *Oxfam International*, October 9. Accessed May 23, 2021. https://oxfamilibrary.openrepository.com/bitstream/handle/10546/620876/bp -human-cost-assam-tea-101019-en.pdf.

Barua, Maan. 2024. *Plantation Worlds*. Durham, NC: Duke University Press.

Baruah, Sanjib. 1986. "Immigration, Ethnic Conflict, and the Political Turmoil—Assam, 1979–1985." *Asian Survey* 26 (11): 1184–1206. doi:10.2307/2644315.

Baruah, Sanjib. 1999. *India Against Itself: Assam and the Politics of Nationality*. Philadelphia: University of Pennsylvania Press.

Baruah, Sanjib. 2020. *In the Name of the Nation: India and Its Northeast*. Palo Alto, CA: Stanford University Press.

Bass, Daniel. 2013. *Everyday Ethnicity in Sri Lanka: Up-Country Tamil Identity Politics*. London: Routledge.

Bates, Crispin, and Alpa Shah, eds. 2014. *Savage Attack: Tribal Insurgency in India*. New Delhi: Social Science Press.

Behal, Rana. 2010. "Coolie Drivers or Benevolent Paternalists? British Tea Planters in Assam and the Indenture Labour System." *Modern Asian Studies* 44 (1): 29–51. doi:10.1017/S0026749X09990059.

Behal, Rana. 2014. *One Hundred Years of Servitude: Political Economy of Tea Plantations in Colonial Assam*. New Delhi: Tulika.

Behal, Rana, and Prabhu Mohapatra. 1992. "'Tea and Money Versus Human Life': The Rise and Fall of the Indenture System in the Assam Tea Plantations 1840–1908." *Journal of Peasant Studies* 19 (3–4): 142–172. doi:10.1080/03066159208438491.

Bertram, Caroline. 2012. "Counting the Poor in India: A Conceptual Analysis of Theory and Praxis of the Government Approach." *South Asia Chronicle* 2:160–188.

Besky, Sarah. 2014. *The Darjeeling Distinction: Labour and Justice on Fair-Trade Tea Plantations in India.* Berkeley: University of California Press.

Besky, Sarah. 2017a. "Fixity: On the Inheritance and Maintenance of Tea Plantation Houses in Darjeeling, India." *American Ethnologist* 44 (4): 617–663. doi:10.1111 /amet.12561.

Besky, Sarah. 2017b. "Tea as 'Hero Crop'? Embodied Algorithms and Industrial Reform in India." *Science as Culture* 26 (1): 11–31. doi:10.1080/09505431.2016.1223110.

Besky, Sarah. 2020. *Tasting Qualities: The Past and Future of Tea.* Berkeley: University of California Press.

Béteille, André. 1998. "The Idea of Indigenous People." *Current Anthropology* 39 (2): 187–192. doi:10.1086/204717.

Bhaumik, Subir. 2012. "India Tea Workers Burn Boss to Death in Assam State." *BBC News.* December 27. Accessed on July 1, 2018. https://www.bbc.com/news/world -asia-india-20849295.

Bhowmik, Sharit. 2011. "Ethnicity and Isolation: Marginalization of Tea Plantation Workers." *Race/Ethnicity: Multidisciplinary Global Contexts* 4 (2): 235–253. doi:10 .2979/racethmulglocon.4.2.235.

Bhowmik, Sharit, Mohammed Abdul Kalam, and Virginius Xaxa, eds. 1996. *Tea Plantation Labour in India.* New Delhi: Friedrich Ebert Stiftung.

Biggs, Eloise M., Niladri Gupta, Sukanya D. Saikia, and John M. A. Duncan. 2018. "The Tea Landscape of Assam: Multi-stakeholder Insights into Sustainable Livelihoods Under a Changing Climate." *Environmental Science & Policy* 82:9–18. doi:10.1016/j.envsci.2018.01.003.

Bora, Bijay Sankar. 2014. "The Killing Fields of Assam." *Tribune*, December 28. http:// www.tribuneindia.com/news/sunday-special/kaleidoscope/the-killing-fields-of -assam/23325.html.

Borah, Kaberi. 2013. "Entrepreneurship in Small Tea Plantations: A Case of Assam." *Echo* 1 (3): 79–90.

Bourdieu, Pierre. 1977. *Outline of a Theory of Practice.* Cambridge: Cambridge University Press.

Bourdieu, Pierre. 1989. "Social Space and Symbolic Power." *Sociological Theory* 7 (1): 14–25. doi:10.2307/202060.

Bourdieu, Pierre. 1998. *Acts of Resistance: Against the Tyranny of the Market.* New York: New Press.

Bourgois, Philipp. 1989. *Ethnicity at Work: Divided Labor on a Central American Banana Plantation.* Baltimore, MD: Johns Hopkins University Press.

Breman, Jan. 1989. *Taming the Coolie Beast: Plantation Society and the Colonial Order in Southeast Asia.* Delhi: Oxford University Press.

Breman, Jan, and Valentine E. Daniel. 1992. "Conclusion: The Making of a Coolie." *The Journal of Peasant Studies* 19(3–4): 268–295. doi: 10.1080/03066159208438496.

Brosius, Christiane. 2016. "Regulating Access and Mobility of Single Women in a 'World Class'-City: Gender and Inequality in Delhi, India." In *Urban Inequality in the Creative City: Issues, Approaches, Comparisons*, edited by Ulrike Gerhard et al., 239–260. New York: Palgrave McMillan.

Brunnegger, Sandra, ed. 2019. *Everyday Justice: Law, Ethnography, Injustice.* Cambridge: Cambridge University Press.

Buechler, Steven M. 1995. "New Social Movement Theories." *Sociological Quarterly* 36 (3): 441–464. doi:10.1111/j.1533-8525.1995.tb00447.x.

Butler, Judith. 2006. *Precarious Life: The Powers of Mourning and Violence.* London: Verso.

Certeau, Michel de. 2013. *The Practice of Everyday Life*. Berkeley: University of California Press.

Chakraborty, Achin, Subhanil Chowdhury, Supurna Banerjee, and Zaad Mahmood, eds. 2019. *Limits of Bargaining: Capital, Labour and the State in Contemporary India*. Cambridge: Cambridge University Press.

Chatterjee, Piya. 2001. *A Time for Tea: Women, Labour, and Post/colonial Politics on an Indian Plantation*. Durham, NC: Duke University Press.

Chaudhuri, Soma. 2013. *Tempest in a Teapot: Witches, Tea Plantations, and Lives of Migrant Labourers in India*. Lanham, MD: Lexington.

Choudhury, Dutta R. 2015. "All State Tea Tribes Not to Get ST Status." *Assam Tribune Online*, February 24. http://www.assamtribune.com/feb2415/at052.txt.

Clarke, Kamari, and Mark Goodale, eds. 2009. *Mirrors of Justice: Law and Power in the Post–Cold War Era*. Cambridge: Cambridge University Press.

Columbia Law School Human Rights Institute. 2014. "'The More Things Change . . .:' The World Bank, Tata and Enduring Abuses on India's Tea Plantations." Accessed May 21, 2020. https://web.law.columbia.edu/sites/default/files/microsites/human-rights-institute/files/tea_report_final_draft-smallpdf.pdf.

Das, Kalyan. 2012. "Tea Smallholdings in Assam: Is There a Way Out?" *Economic and Political Weekly* 47 (11): 23–25.

Das, Veena. 2007. *Life and Words: Violence and the Descent into the Ordinary*. Berkeley: University of California Press.

Das, Veena. 2012. "Ordinary Ethics." In *A Companion to Moral Anthropology*, edited by Didier Fassin, 133–149. Malden, MA: Wiley.

Das, Veena. 2018a. "Ethics, Self-Knowledge, and Life Taken as a Whole." *Hau: Journal of Ethnographic Theory* 8 (3): 537–549.

Das, Veena. 2018b. "On Singularity and the Event: Further Reflections on the Ordinary." In *Recovering the Human Subject: Freedom, Creativity and Decision*, edited by James Laidlaw, 53–73. Cambridge: Cambridge University Press.

Das, Veena. 2020. *Textures of the Ordinary: Doing Anthropology After Wittgenstein*. New York: Fordham University Press.

Davis, Janae, Alex A. Moulton, Levi Van Sant, and Brian Williams. 2019. "Anthropocene, Capitalocene, . . . Plantationocene?: A Manifesto for Ecological Justice in an Age of Global Crisis." *Geography Compass* 13 (5): e12438. doi:10.1111/gec3.12438.

Della Porta, Donatella, and Mario Diani. 2006. *Social Movements: An Introduction*. Malden, MA: Blackwell.

Deshpande, Ashwini. 2013. *Affirmative Action in India*. New Delhi: Oxford University Press.

DiAngelo, Robin. 2018. White Fragility: Why It's so Hard for White People to Talk about Racism. Boston: Beacon Press.

Dumm, Thomas L. 1999. *A Politics of the Ordinary*. New York: New York University Press.

Eckert, Julia M. 2002. "Der Hindunationalismus und die Politik der Unverhandelbarkeit: Vom politischen Nutzen eines vermeintlichen Religionskonfliktes." *Politik und Zeitgeschichte* 52 (42–43): 23–30.

Eckert, Julia M. 2011. "Subjects of Citizenship." *Citizenship Studies* 15 (3–4): 309–317.

Eckert, Julia M. 2020. *The Bureaucratic Production of Difference: Ethos and Ethics in Migration Administrations*. Bielefeld: transcript.

Eckert, Julia M. 2023. "Decolonising the Political: Presence, Law and Obligation." *Anthropological Theory* 23 (4): 436–458.

Eidson, John R., Dereje Feyissa, Veronika Fuest, Markus Hoehne, Boris Nieswand, Günther Schlee, and Olaf Zenker. 2017. "From Identification to Framing and Alignment: A New Approach to the Comparative Analysis of Collective Identities." *Current Anthropology* 58 (3): S340–59. doi:10.1086/691970.

Ferguson, James. 2013. "Declarations of Dependence: Labour, Personhood, and Welfare in Southern Africa." *Journal of the Royal Anthropological Institute* 19 (2): 223–242.

Fernandes, Walter. 2003. "Assam Adivasis: Identity Issues and Liberation." *Vidyajyoti Journal of Theological Reflection.* Accessed September 5, 2023. https://www.vidyajyotijournal.com/.

Fraser, Nancy. 2010. *Scales of Justice: Reimagining Political Space in a Globalizing World.* New York: Columbia University Press.

Fraser, Nancy, and Axel Honneth. 2003. *Redistribution or Recognition? A Political-Philosophical Exchange.* London: Verso.

Giddens, Anthony. 1984. *The Constitution of Society: Outline of the Theory of Structuration.* Berkeley: University of California Press.

Government of India. 2005. *National Commission for Scheduled Tribes: A Handbook.* New Delhi: Government of India.

Griffiths, Percival. 1967. *The History of the Indian Tea Industry.* London: Weidenfeld & Nicolson.

Guha, Amalendu. (1977) 2016. *Planter Raj to Swaraj: Freedom Struggle and Electoral Politics in Assam, 1826–1947.* New Delhi: Tulika.

Guha, Ramachandra. (2007) 2008. *India After Gandhi: The History of the World's Largest Democracy.* London: Pan.

Gurr, Ted Robert. 1970. *Why Men Rebel.* Princeton, NJ: Princeton University Press.

Haraway, Donna. 2015. "Anthropocene, Capitalocene, Plantationocene, Chthulucene: Making Kin." *Environmental Humanities* 6 (1): 159–165. doi:10.1215/22011919-3615934.

Haraway, Donna, Noboru Ishikawa, Scott F. Gilbert, Kenneth Olwig, Anna L. Tsing, and Nils Bubandt. 2016. "Anthropologists Are Talking—About the Anthropocene." *Ethnos* 81 (3): 535–564. doi:10.1080/00141844.2015.1105838.

Harrison, Faye V., ed. 1991. *Decolonizing Anthropology: Moving Further toward an Anthropology of Liberation.* Arlington, VA: American Anthropological Association.

Holbraad, Martin. 2012. *Truth in Motion: The Recursive Anthropology of Cuban Divination.* Chicago: University of Chicago Press.

ILO (International Labour Organization). 2017. *Minimum Wage Policy Guide: A Summary.* October 18. Accessed July 2, 2018. https://www.ilo.org/wcmsp5/groups/public/---dgreports/---dcomm/---publ/documents/publication/wcms_570376.pdf.

International Work Group for Indigenous Affairs. 2021. *The Indigenous World 2021.* Accessed July 25, 2022. https://www.iwgia.org/en/resources/indigenous-world.html.

Ives, Sarah. 2017. *Steeped in Heritage: The Racial Politics of South African Rooibos Tea.* Durham, NC: Duke University Press.

Jegathesan, Mythri. 2019. *Tea and Solidarity: Tamil Women and Work in Postwar Sri Lanka.* Seattle: University of Washington Press.

Jegathesan, Mythri. 2021. "Black Feminist Plots Before the Plantationocene and Anthropology's 'Regional Closets.'" *Feminist Anthropology* 2 (1): 78–93. doi:10.1002/fea2.12037.

Johnson, Jessica, and George Hamandishe Karekwaivanane, eds. 2018. *Pursuing Justice in Africa: Competing Imaginaries and Contested Practices.* Athens: Ohio University Press.

Kannuri, Nanda Kishore, and Sushrut Jadhav. 2021. "Cultivating Distress: Cotton, Caste, and Farmer Suicides in India." *Anthropology & Medicine* 28 (4): 558–575. doi:10.1080/13648470.2021.1993630.

Kantor, Hayden S. 2020. "Locating the Farmer: Ideologies of Agricultural Labor in Bihar, India." *Anthropology of Work Review* 41 (2): 97–107. doi:10.1111/awr.12208.

Karlsson, Bengt G., and T. B. Subba, eds. 2006. *Indigeneity in India*. London: Kegan Paul.

Kelly, Tobias. 2008. "The Attractions of Accountancy: Living an Ordinary Life During the Second Palestinian Intifada." *Ethnography* 9 (3): 351–376.

Khan, Naveeda. 2010. "Mosque Construction or the Violence of the Ordinary." In *Beyond Crisis: Re-evaluating Pakistan*, edited by Naveeda Khan, 428–520. New Delhi: Routledge.

Kikon, Dolly. 2017. "Jackfruit Seeds from Jharkhand: Being Adivasi in Assam." *Contributions to Indian Sociology* 51 (3): 313–337. doi:10.1177%2F0069966717720575.

Kikon, Dolly, and Bengt G. Karlsson. 2019. *Leaving the Land: Indigenous Migration and Affective Labour in India*. Cambridge: Cambridge University Press.

Kowal, Sabine, and Daniel C. O'Connell. 2012. "Zur Transkription von Gesprächen." In *Qualitative Forschung. Ein Handbuch*, edited by Uwe Flick et al., 437–447. Reinbek: Rowohlt.

Kulke, Hermann, and Dietmar Rothermund. 1998. Geschichte Indiens. Von der Induskultur bis heute. München: Beck.

Kumar, Arvind. 2023. "Exclusion of Pasmanda Muslims and Dalit Christians from the Scheduled Caste Quota." *South Asia Research* 43 (2): 192–209. https://doi.org/10.1177/02627280231161000.

Kumpf, Desirée. 2020. "Organic Taste and Labour on Indian Tea Plantations." *Social Anthropology* 28 (4): 789–802. doi:10.1111/1469-8676.12951.

Lahiri, Souparna. 2000. "Bonded Labour and the Tea Plantation Economy." *Revolutionary Democracy* 6 (2). Accessed May 21, 2020. http://www.revolutionarydemocracy.org/rdv6n2/tea.htmay.

Latour, Bruno. 2005. *Reassembling the Social: An Introduction to Actor-Network-Theory*. Oxford: Oxford University Press.

Lefebvre, Henri. 2014. *Critique of Everyday Life*. London: Verso.

Lethabo King, Tiffany. 2019. *The Black Shoals: Offshore Formations of Black and Native Studies*. Durham, NC: Duke University Press.

Malinowski, Bronislaw. 1922. *Argonauts of the Western Pacific: An Account of Native Enterprise and Adventure in the Archipelagoes of Melanesian New Guinea*. London: Routledge & Kegan Paul.

Marcus, George. 1993. "Mass Toxic Torts and the End of Everyday Life." In *Law in Everyday Life*, edited by Austin Sarat and Thomas Kearns, 237–274. Ann Arbor: University of Michigan Press.

McKittrick, Katherine. 2013. "Plantation Futures." *Small Axe* 17 (3): 1–15.

Michaels, Axel. 2012. *Der Hinduismus: Geschichte und Gegenwart*. München: Beck.

Middleton, Townsend. 2013. "Scheduling Tribes: A View from Inside India's Ethnographic State." *Focaal* 65 (2013): 13–22. doi:10.3167/fcl.2013.650102.

Millar, Kathleen M. 2017. "Toward a Critical Politics of Precarity." *Sociology Compass* 11 (6): e12483. doi:10.1111/soc4.12483.

Ministry of Labour and Employment. 2008. *Report on the Working of the Minimum Wages Act, 1948*. Chandigarh: Labour Bureau.

Ministry of Tribal Affairs. 2019. *State/Union Territory-wise List of Scheduled Tribes in India*. Accessed July 22, 2021. https://tribal.nic.in/ST/LatestListofScheduledtribes.pdf.

Mishra, Deepak K., Atul Sarma, and Vandana Upadhyay. 2012. *Unfolding Crisis in Assam's Tea Plantations: Employment and Occupational Mobility*. Delhi: Routledge.

Nagar, Anirudha, and Francesca Feruglio. 2016. "World Bank Investment on Assam's Tea Plantations: Hearing the Voices of Workers?" *Open Democracy*, October 4.

Accessed May 25, 2020. https://www.opendemocracy.net/beyondslavery/franc esca-feruglio-anirudha-nagar/world-bank-investment-on-assam-s-tea-planta tions-hea.

Nawa Bihan Samaj. 2013. "No ST No Rest." *Adivasi Avaz* 18 (May–June): 35–36.

Nilsen, Alf Gunvald. 2012. "Adivasis in and Against the State." *Critical Asian Studies* 44 (2): 251–282. doi:10.1080/14672715.2012.672827.

Nussbaum, Martha. 2011. "Foreword." In *Responsibility of Justice*, authored by Iris Marion Young, ix–xxvi. Oxford: Oxford University Press.

O'Hanlon, Rosalind. 1988. "Recovering the Subject: Subaltern Studies and Histories of Resistance in Colonial South Asia." *Modern Asian Studies* 22 (1): 189–224. doi:10.1017/S0026749X00009471.

Parmar, Pooja. 2016. *Indigeneity and Legal Pluralism in India: Claims, Histories, Meanings*. Delhi: Cambridge University Press.

Paulson, Steve. 2019. "Making Kin: An Interview with Donna Haraway." *Los Angeles Review of Books*, December 6. Accessed December 28, 2021. https://www.lare viewofbooks.org/article/making-kin-an-interview-with-donna-haraway/.

Raj, Jayaseelan. 2013. "Alienated Enclaves: Economic Crisis and Neo-Bondage in a South Indian Plantation Belt." *Forum for Development Studies* 40 (3): 465–490. doi:10.1080/08039410.2013.799098.

Raj, Jayaseelan. 2022. *Plantation Crisis: Ruptures of Dalit Life in the Indian Tea Belt*. London: UCL Press.

Rajya Sabha (Department Related Parliamentary Standing Committee on Commerce). 2012. "Performance of Plantation Sector—Tea and Coffee Industry." Report No. 102. New Delhi: Rajya Sabha Secretariat.

Raman, Ravi K. (2010) 2015. *Global Capital and Peripheral Labour: The History and Political Economy of Plantation Workers in India*. Milton Park: Routledge.

Ray, Pramita. 2016. "Tainted Tea: Slave Labour in Your Cuppa?" *Cividep India*. Report, May 4. http://www.forumfor.no/assets/docs/Tainted-Tea-Report.pdf.

Reddy, Narasimha, and Srijit Mishra, eds. 2012. *Agrarian Crisis in India*. New Delhi: Oxford University Press.

Reemtsma, Jan Philipp. 1999. Das Recht des Opfers auf die Bestrafung des Täters - als Problem. München: C. H. Beck.

Rowlatt, Justine, and Jane Deith. 2015. "The Bitter Story Behind the UK's National Drink." *BBC News*, September 8. http://www.bbc.com/news/world-asia-india-34 173532.

Sanchez, Andrew, and Christian Strümpell. 2014. "Sons of Soil, Sons of Steel: Autochthony, Descent and the Class Concept in Industrial India." *Modern Asian Studies* 48 (5): 1276–1301. doi:10.1017/S0026749X14000213.

Scott, James. 1976. *The Moral Economy of the Peasant: Subsistence and Rebellion in Southeast Asia*. New Haven, CT: Yale University Press.

Scott, James. 1985. *Weapons of the Weak: Everyday Forms of Peasant Resistance*. New Haven, CT: Yale University Press.

Scott, James C. 1990. *Domination and the Arts of Resistance: Hidden Transcripts*. New Haven, CT: Yale University Press.

Sen, Debarati. 2017. *Everyday Sustainability: Gender Justice and Fair Trade Tea in Darjeeling*. Albany: State University of New York Press.

Shah, Alpa. 2010. *In the Shadows of the State: Indigenous Politics, Environmentalism and Insurgency in Jharkhand*. Durham, NC: Duke University Press.

Shah, Alpa, and Sara Shneiderman. 2013. "The Practices, Policies, and Politics of Transforming Inequality in South Asia: Ethnographies of Affirmative Action." *Focaal* 65 (2013): 3–12. doi:10.3167/fcl.2013.650101.

Sharma, Ashmita, and Saqib Khan. 2018. "The Paradox of Indigeneity: Adivasi Struggle for ST Status in Assam." *Contributions to Indian Sociology* 52 (2): 186–211. doi:10.1177/0069966718761746.

Sharma, Jayeeta. 2011. *Empire's Garden: Assam and the Making of India*. Durham, NC: Duke University Press.

Singh, Bikash. 2020. "Repealing of Plantation Labour Act 1951 Will Affect the Tea Industry: Tea Association of India." *Economic Times*, January 25. https://economic times.indiatimes.com/news/economy/agriculture/repealing-of-plantation-labour -act-1951-will-affect-the-tea-industry-tea-association-of-india/articleshow /73614509.cms?from=mdr.

Spivak, Gayatri. 1988. *In Other Worlds: Essays in Cultural Politics*. New York: Methuen.

Starr, Gerald. 1981. *Minimum Wage Fixing: An International Review of Practices and Problems*. Geneva: International Labour Organisation.

Steur, Luisa. 2014. "An 'Expanded' Class Perspective: Bringing Capitalism Down to Earth in the Changing Political Lives of Adivasi Workers in Kerala." *Modern Asian Studies* 48 (5): 1334–1357. doi:10.1017/S0026749X14000407.

Stoler, Ann Laura. 1985. *Capitalism and Confrontation in Sumatra's Plantation Belt, 1870–1979*. New Haven, CT: Yale University Press.

Tea Board of India. 2017. *63rd Annual Report, 2016–2017*. Kolkata: Saraswaty. (Government of West Bengal Enterprise). Accessed March 14, 2022. http://teaboard.gov .in/pdf/Annual_Report_Combined_2016_17_Total_Book_27_11_2017_Final _Curve_pdf4622.pdf.

Tea Board of India. 2022. *State/Region Wise and Month Wise Tea Production Data for the Year 2022*. Accessed September 9, 2024. https://www.teaboard.gov.in/pdf /Production_2022_and_2022_23_pdf5959.pdf.

Thompson, E. P. 1971. "The Moral Economy of the English Crowd in the Eighteenth Century." *Past & Present* (50): 76–136. https://www.jstor.org/stable/650244.

Times of India. 2015. "Tea Gardens Should Give Minimum Wage of 169: CM." Accessed September 5, 2024. https://timesofindia.indiatimes.com/city/guwahati/tea-gardens -should-give-minimum-wage-of-rs-169-cm/articleshow/45925893.cms.

Varma, Nitin. 2011. "Coolie Strikes Back: Protest and Collective Action in the Colonial Tea Plantations of Assam." In *Adivasis in Colonial India: Survival, Resistance and Negotiation*, edited by Biswamoy Pati, 86–215. New Delhi: Orient Blackswan.

Varma, Nitin. 2016. *Coolies of Capitalism: Assam Tea and the Making of Coolie Labour*. Berlin: De Gruyter Oldenbourg.

Viveiros de Castro, E. 1998. "Cosmological Deixis and Amerindian Perspectivism." *Journal of the Royal Anthropological Institute* 4:469–488. doi:10.2307/3034157.

Weiner, Myron. 1983. "The Political Demography of Assam's Anti-Immigrant Movement." *Population and Development Review* 9 (2): 279–292.

Wekker, Gloria. 2016. *White Innocence: Paradoxes of Colonialism and Race*. Durham, NC: Duke University Press.

Wenner, Miriam. 2013. "Challenging the State by Reproducing Its Principles: The Demand for 'Gorkhaland' between Regional Autonomy and the National Belonging." *Asian Ethnology* 72 (2): 199–220. doi:10.5167/uzh-87966.

Willford, Andrew C. 2014. *Tamils and the Haunting of Justice: History and Recognition in Malaysia's Plantations*. Honolulu: University of Hawaii Press.

Williams, Raymond. 1980. *Problems in Materialism and Culture: Selected Essays*. London: Verso.

Wimmer, Andreas, and Nina Glick Schiller. 2002. "Methodological Nationalism and Beyond: Nation-State Building, Migration and the Social Sciences." *Global Networks* 2 (4): 301–334. doi:10.1111/1471-0374.00043.

Wolford, Wendy. 2021. "The Plantationocene: A Lusotropical Contribution to the Theory." *Annals of the American Association of Geographers* 111 (6): 1622–1639. doi:10.1080/24694452.2020.1850231.

Wright, Fiona. (2016) 2023. "Resistance." In *The Open Encyclopedia of Anthropology*, edited by Felix Stein. doi:10.29164/16resistance.

Xaxa, Virginius. 1996. "Condition of Tea Estate Labourers in Assam." In *Tea Plantation Labour in India*, edited by Sharit Bhowmik, Mohammed Kalam, and Virginius Xaxa, 15–42. New Delhi: Friedrich Ebert Stiftung.

Xaxa, Virginius. 2014. *State, Society and Tribes: Issues in Post-Colonial India*. Noida: Pearson.

Young, Iris Marion. 2011. *Responsibility for Justice*. New York: Oxford University Press.

Zenker, Olaf. 2011. "Autochthony, Ethnicity, Indigeneity and Nationalism: Time-Honouring and State-Oriented Modes of Rooting Individual-Territory-Group Triads in a Globalizing World." *Critique of Anthropology* 31 (1): 63–81. doi:10.1177/0308275X10393438.

Zenker, Olaf. 2016. "Anthropology on Trial: Exploring the Laws of Anthropological Expertise." *International Journal of Law in Context* 12 (3): 293–311. doi:10.1017/S174455231600015X.

Zenker, Olaf. 2018. "Why the Individual Must be Defended—Seemingly Against All Anthropological Odds." In *Personal Autonomy in Plural Societies: A Principle and Its Paradoxes*, edited by Marie-Claire Foblets, Michele Graziadei, and Alison Dundes Renteln, 98–111. London: Routledge.

Zenker, Olaf. 2022. "Politics of Belonging." In *Oxford Handbook of Law and Anthropology*, edited by Marie-Claire Foblets, Mark Goodale, Maria Sapignoli, and Olaf Zenker, 772–791. Oxford: Oxford University Press.

Zenker, Olaf, and Anna-Lena Wolf. 2024. "Towards a New Anthropology of Justice in the Anthropocene: Anthropological (Re)turns." *Zeitschrift für Ethnologie | Journal of Social and Cultural Anthropology* 149(2): 189–216.

Index

Act VI of the Bengal Council (1865), 27, 59
Adivasis
    activism of, 34, 72–73, 77–79, 111
    and casteism and economic precarity, 36
    categorization of, 19–20, 21
    in plantation labor force, 19, 117n17
    Jaipal Singh's importance in politics of,
        118n27
    and situational adaptations of collective
        identities, 83–85, 87
Adivasi Welfare and Development Council,
    120n10
affirmative action, 77–79, 120n5
agency, 9–10, 58
All Adivasi Students' Association of Assam
    (AASAA), 77, 84
All Assam Students Union (AASU), 96
All Assam Tea Tribes Student Association
    (ATTSA), 82, 84, 85
All India Trade Union Congress (AITUC), 74
Amalgamated Plantations Private Limited
    (APPL), 17, 120n3
amenities
    for laborers, 99–101, 111–12, 119n3
    and minimum wage, 76, 103–5
    for tea planters, 3, 92–95
Anglo-Burmese war, 12
Assam Accord, 96
Assam Chah-Bagan Mazdoor Union, 75
Assam Chah Mazdoor Sangha (ACMS)
    availability of leadership positions in, 85
    bilateral agreements between Consultative
        Committee of Plantation Associations
        and, 15, 117n22
    and old-style plantation economy, 75–77
    and social mobility, 34
    and wage increase negotiations, 2, 15,
        80–81, 82
Assam Company, 12
Assamese, 117n20
Assam Gana Sangram Parishad (AGSP), 96
Assam Mazdoor Union, 77
Assam movement, 96
Assam Provincial Trade Union Congress
    (APTUC), 74–75

Assam Tea Tribes Student Association, 34
auction system, 101–2

bāgāniyā, 21, 83
bāgān ke log, 21, 83
Banerjee, Supurna, 10, 33–34, 91
Baruah, Sanjib, 11, 19, 96
Behal, Rana, 21, 31, 59, 60–61, 69, 74, 75,
    90–92
benefits
    for laborers, 99–101, 111–12, 119n3
    and minimum wage, 76, 103–5
    for tea planters, 3, 92–95
benevolence, of tea planters, 89–91
Bengalis, 14, 92, 117n20
Bentinck, Lord, 12
Besky, Sarah, 4–5, 6, 8, 9–10, 35, 91
Bharatiya Janata Party (BJP), 119n2
Bhartiya Chah Mazdoor Sangha, 119n2
Bhowmik, Sharit, 35
bisnis model of plantation economy, 6, 115n8
Bodos, 83–84
bonded labor, 15, 35–36 See also modern-day
    slavery, neo-bondage
Borah, Kaberi, 17
Bought Leaf Factory (BLF), 17, 101
Bourdieu, Pierre, 86, 118n3
Bruce, Charles, 12
Bruce, Robert, 12
Brunnegger, Sandra, 9, 39, 108, 116n12
bungalow doctrine, 88, 105, 111
Butler, Judith, 118n3

Cachar Chah Sramik Union, 119n2
caste hierarchies, blurring of, 25
casteism, 36, 38, 88, 99–105, 106, 112, 118n7
Central Wage Board, 15
Charlton, Andrew, 12
Charter Act of 1833, 12–13
child labor, 74, 119n5
Child Labour (Prohibition and Regulation)
    Act (1986), 119n5
Chota Nagpuri Association, 74
Chotanagpur Plateau, 13, 28, 59
cities, temporary migration to, 33

classism, 88, 99–105, 106, 112
Code on Occupational Safety, Health and
    Working Conditions, 18, 82
collective identification, 72–74, 86–87, 110–11
    and Adivasis' fight for affirmative action,
        77–79
    and campaign for statutory minimum wage,
        80–82
    and old-style plantation economy, 74–77
    situational adaptations of, 82–86
    See also labor rights; labor unions
Consultative Committee of Plantation
    Associations (CCPA), 15, 75, 82, 102,
    117n22
coolie drivers, 90
crush, tear, curl (CTC) black tea, 49–50
CTC processing, 49–50

Dalits, 19, 36, 117n24, 119n8
Darjeeling Distinction, The (Besky), 4–5
debt, 98
Defense of India Rules, 74
desertion, 59, 60
desire, 8–9
"dignified work," 64
dignity, 62, 64. *See also* humanity
disability rights, 68–69
discrimination, and indigeneity, 79
distributive justice, 66–67
dual wage structure, 3, 18, 70, 82

East India Company, 11–12
Economically Weaker Sections (EWS), 20
education, 43
enclave perspective, 26, 34–38, 108
endogamy, 117n17
Equal Remuneration Act (1975), 15
everyday, 39–40. *See also* ordinariness
everyday justice, 39, 116n12
everyday life, maintaining, 53–54
everyday resistance, 39, 61–62 *See also*
    resistance
Everyday Sustainability (Sen), 5
exoduses, 60–61
"ex–tea tribes," 21, 31, 73, 82, 83

Fair Trade, 4, 5, 6, 115n10
farming
    and labor migration, 31–32, 37
    and supplemental income, 29
Fassin, Didier, 116n15
Fernandes, Walter, 117n17
Fisher, Josh, 64

fixity, 35–36
food rations, 1, 32, 104–5, 119n3
Foreign Exchange Management Act (FEMA,
    2000), 16
Foreign Exchange Regulation Act (FERA,
    1973), 16, 92
Fraser, Nancy, 26

Gandhi, Mahatma, 60
gendered nature of plantation work and life,
    54–55
gendered projects of value, 5, 8
gender justice, 6, 8
"Gerechtigkeitsgefühl" (feelings of justice), 64,
    119n2
Giddens, Anthony, 10
Gorkha, 115n7
Gorkhaland movement, 4, 115n7
Great Depression, 61
Griffiths, Percival, 89–90

Haraway, Donna, 36, 118n6
hegemonic order, maintaining rather than
    subverting, 58
Heidegger, Martin, 6
hierarchy, 25, 58, 63–64
Hindustan Unilever, 17, 98
housework, 53–54
housing, 62
humanity
    and resistance, 63
    See also dignity
human rights, 33, 34, 63, 109
human trafficking, 33, 52–53
hundi, 52–53, 119n2

immigration, 96–97
indentured labor regime, 13–14, 27–28, 37,
    59, 60
Indian National Trade Union Congress
    (INTUC), 75
Indian Tea Association, 13, 27
Indian Trade Union Movement, 74
indigeneity, 19–20, 78–79, 111. *See also*
    Adivasis
Indo-Aryan migration theory, 19–20
industri model of plantation economy, 58,
    115n8
"insider-outsider," 22–23
International Labour Organization, 80

Jalan, Avantika, 120n4
Jalan, Murleidhor, 99, 117n19

jāti, 25, 83, 118n1
Jegathesan, Mythri, 5–6, 8, 33, 37, 116n11
justice
    analytical definition of, 7, 8
    distributive, 66–67
    in human rights discourse, 109
    laborers' identification and shifting visions
        of, 82–86
    new anthropology of, 116n12
    objects of, 7, 8, 10–11, 58, 70, 86–87, 108–11
    in research on industrial tea production,
        4–7
    resistance and transformation of working
        modes of, 69–71
    and revenge, 64
    subjects of, 7, 8, 9, 11, 70, 85–86, 87, 99,
        109–11
    tea planters' responsibility for, 106–7
    upscaling, 10, 26, 38, 108–9
justice at work, 3–4, 7, 9–11, 24, 58, 108–113
justice imaginaries, 5–6, 8–11, 23–24, 38, 61,
    69, 73, 87–88, 99–105, 110–112
justice in conflict, 10, 11, 24, 106–7, 112.
justice in context, 10–11, 23–24, 40, 58, 69–71,
    110
justice in transition, 10–11, 86–87, 110–11
justice on scales, 10–11, 23, 26, 38, 108–110

Kelly, Tobias, 119n1
Kenya, 16, 117n23
Khan, Naveeda, 29
Khondos, 83
killer stories, 39
King, Tiffany Lethabo, 37
Koch-Rajbonshi, 79

labor conditions, 14–18, 99–101
labor contracts, 18, 28, 30–31, 77, 110
laborers
    amenities for, 14–18, 99–101, 111–12, 119n3
    designations of, 19–21
    justice imaginaries of, 58, 61–71, 110
    recruitment of, 13–14, 25, 27–29, 33, 59
labor migration
    history of, 27–31
    postcolonial, 31–34, 37
labor recruitment, 13–14, 25, 27–29, 33, 59
labor rights, 37, 109, 110–11, 120n3. *See also*
    labor unions
labor unions, 34, 36, 61, 68, 74–77, 120n3
Lahiri, Souparna, 35
"law, exploitation of," 104–5
loyalty, 55, 56–71. *See also* resistance

Malinowski, Bronislaw, 88
Marwaris, 96–97, 99, 117n20
maternity leave, 103–4
"methodological enclavism," 23, 34–38
Middleton, Townsend, 79
Miller, David Leslie, 116n14
minimum wage, 2, 15, 72, 76–77, 80–82,
    102–5, 112–13. *See also* wages
Minimum Wage Advisory Committee, 15
Minimum Wages Act (1948), 14–15, 80
Mishra, Deepak K., 34–35, 119n5
mobility. *See* labor migration; social mobility;
    spatial mobility
modern-day slavery, 3, 15, 27, 34–38. *See also*
    neo-bondage, bonded labor
mohara, 47–48, 57
moral economy, 5, 77, 116n15.

neo-bondage, 35–36
noncooperation movement, 60

objects of justice, 7, 8, 10–11, 58, 70, 86–87,
    108–11
Odia, 84, 85, 120n9
"old-style" plantation economy, 3, 14–15, 36,
    38, 40, 55, 58, 70–71, 74–77, 110, 113
opium, 12
Oram, Juel, 79
ordinariness, 39–40. *See also* everyday
orthodox tea, 50
Other Backward Classes (OBC), 20–21,
    76, 79

penal contract system, 27–28, 60
People's Action for Development, 77
plantation crisis, 16, 30, 35, 98, 117n24
plantation economies
    research on, 4–7, 9–10
    See also "old-style" plantation economy
plantation enclaves, 23, 26–27, 34–38,
    108, 113
Plantationocene, 36–37, 118n6
plantations
    composition of labor force on, 19,
        117n17
    futures of, 112–13
    labor migration away from, in postcolonial
        times, 31–34
    loyalty toward, 55, 56–71
    ownership of, 16–17
    as permeable spaces, 26–27, 34–37
    statistical information on, 117n25,
        119n5

Plantations Labour Act (PLA, 1951)
amendments of, 117n21
justice imaginaries based on, 18, 77, 99
and bondage, 15
and "old-style" plantation economy, 14–15, 58, 70–71, 77
replacement of, with Code on Occupational Safety, Health and Working Conditions, 18, 82
wages under, 3, 14–15
planters. *See* tea planters
plucking tea leaves, 45–47
poiēsis of desire, 6–9, 37
political economy, 11–19, 31–32, 36, 38, 70–71, 77, 98, 108, 110, 112–13
positionality, 115n6
postcolonial labor migration, 28–31
precarity, 26, 30–31, 36, 37, 118n3
profits, maximization of, 88
protest(s). *See* resistance
pruning, 56–57, 61–62, 64–66

racism, structural, 118n7
Raj, Jayaseelan, 9, 35, 36, 117n24, 119n8
"Rechtsgefühle" (legal feelings), 119n2
Reemtsma, Jan Philipp, 64, 119n2
resistance, 57–58
agency as, 10, 58
analysis of instances of, 61–69
histories of tea labor, 59–61
and transformation of working modes of justice, 69–71
responsible agents of justice, 7, 9, 11, 26. *See also* tea planters
revenge, 60, 64
rewards, 66–67

Sarma, Atul, 34–35
Sarwan, P. M., 74
Scheduled Castes, 20
Scheduled Tribes (ST), 20–21, 73, 77–79, 84–86, 111. *See also* Adivasis
Schiller, Nina Glick, 37–38
Scott, James C., 5, 57, 61, 69, 119n1
seasons, 56
security threats, against managers, 96
Sen, Debarati, 5, 8, 22, 115nn9–10, 119n2
Sharma, A., 29, 117n25
Singh, Jaipal, 20, 118n27
sirdars / sardars, 28–29, 56–57, 61–62
slavery, 13, 27. *See also* modern-day slavery
small tea grower, 5, 17, 77, 110, 112
social mobility, 32–34, 37, 105, 108–9, 113

Soviet Union, 16
spatial mobility, 32–34, 37, 113
Spivak, Gayatri, 120n11
Stoler, Ann, 9
strategic essentialism, 86, 120n11
Structural Adjustment Programs, 117n23
structural casteism, 36, 38, 88, 106, 118n7
structural classism, 88, 106
structural racism, 118n7
subjects of justice, 7, 8, 9, 11, 70, 85–86, 87, 99, 109–11
subsistence ethic, 68, 69
subsistence farming, 13, 29, 31, 32, 37
suffering, reciprocal infliction of, 64
sustainability, 5, 6, 115n9
swaccha vyāpār, 5, 6, 115n10

Tanti, Dileswar, 2, 76
Tata Consumer Products Limited, 17, 30, 98, 120n3
Tea & Solidarity (Jegathesan), 5–6
tea auction system, 101–2
Tea Committee, 12
tea crisis, 9, 16, 30, 35, 98
tea leaf weighing, 47–48, 51
"tea mania," 120n1
Tea Marketing Control Order (1984), 101
tea planters, 88–89, 106–7
ambivalent character of, in relation to plantation laborers, 89–91, 111–12
justice imaginaries of, 99–105
lifestyle of, 3, 92–93
as no-longer-desirable occupation, 97–98
position in tea industry, 91–92
responsibilities and challenges of, 94–97, 98
use of term, 115n5
See also responsible agents of justice
tea plucking, 45–47
tea selling, 101–2
tea tasting, 101–2
"tea tribes," 21, 73, 82–84, 87, 111
Teekampagne, 106
Thai-Ahom, 79, 111
"Third World agrarian imaginary," 4
Thompson, E. P., 5, 77, 116n15
trade unions, 34, 36, 61, 68, 74–77, 120n3.
Tripartite Committee of the 15th Indian Labour Conference (1957), 81–82
tripartite moral economy, 4, 6, 8, 9–10

unbecoming labor, 6
unions. *See* trade unions
United Liberation Front of Assam, 96

Universal Declaration of Human Rights
  (1948), 109
unregistered labor recruitment, 28
UN Working Group on Indigenous
  Populations, 86
Upadhyay, Vandana, 34–35
upscaling justice, 10, 26, 38, 108–9

"Vanvasis," 20. *See also* Adivasis
violence, resistance through acts of, 59–60,
  63–64

wages, 14–15, 68, 69, 106, 115n4, 120n8. *See
  also* minimum wage
Wasteland Rules of 1838, 13

weighing tea leaves, 47–48, 51
Willford, Andrew C., 18
Wimmer, Andreas, 37–38
women
  gendered nature of plantation work and life,
    54–55
  gendered projects of value, 8
  gender justice, 6, 8
  smallholder women tea farmers, 115n10
Workmen's Breach of Contract Act (1859),
  27–28, 59, 60

Young, Iris, 106

Zenker, Olaf, 7, 120n11

www.ingramcontent.com/pod-product-compliance
Lightning Source LLC
Chambersburg PA
CBHW030603270326
41927CB00007B/1031